Received in Grace

Received in Grace

The Search for a Birth Family

Norman M. Carson

Writers Club Press
San Jose New York Lincoln Shanghai

Received in Grace
The Search for a Birth Family

Writers Club Press
an imprint of iUniverse.com, Inc.

For information address:
iUniverse.com, Inc.
5220 S 16th, Ste. 200
Lincoln, NE 68512
www.iuniverse.com

ISBN: 0-595-19973-9

Printed in the United States of America

To Beverly my loving wife,
encourager and dauntless fellow detective.

I wish to thank Professors S. S. Hanna and Harry Farra for their constant encouragement; Drew and Lynne Gordon for their proofreading skills; and for Jane Klein whose expert assistance proved to be invaluable.

Contents

Introduction

The Toronto skyline, dominated by the CN Tower, stretched out before us. My wife and I were in the midst of a leisurely dinner that we were sharing with Carol and John, two of my former students. Carol, an intense and extremely bright young woman, had reached the midpoint of her personal story.

"Well," she said ruefully, "it didn't turn out to be anything like I had expected. In fact," she added, her face darkening, "it was really a bad scene."

She paused, and to encourage her, I said, "I've heard that your experience isn't all that unusual. Many adoptees find the whole experience to be anything but pleasant." I continued. "Still, something good may come of it, despite your initial contacts."

Carol smiled, and John expressed his opinion that she should keep at it just a little longer. "Someone in your family might turn out to be the person who will make it all worthwhile."

"I'm not so sure," Carol said. "It's so very discouraging." She turned to me. "I hope that my bad experience isn't turning you off."

"I've been warned," I said. "Ever since I really began to think seriously about searching for *my* family, more people have taken a negative than a positive approach. They corroborate your testimony: 'It's bound to be a bad scene,' they say. And it's not just the old saw about finding that you have a highwayman for a great-great grandfather." I could see by the pain in Carol's eyes that she fully agreed.

"It is worse, much worse!" She turned to me. "Are you going to pursue your dream anyway?"

"I am," I said, "and let the chips fall where they may."

I did pursue my dream and I let the chips fall. This, then, is my story, the tale of a dream pursued. It is not only a narrative tale; it is also an exemplum of a doctrine of the Christian Faith, the doctrine of adoption in Christ. I trust that it will succeed on both counts.

1

A Contented Child

Sometime in the fifty-ninth year of my life I sat, half naked, on the examining table in my internist's office, wrapping up my annual physical examination. Being a curious creature, it was my habit to ask miscellaneous questions of the doctor. I felt free to do so for he had been my college classmate.

"David," I asked, "should I start jogging every day? I do play some tennis, but I wonder if I wouldn't get more benefit out of something more extreme."

"Did your Dad run daily," he asked, "or even weekly?"

I admitted that my father had seldom made it his practice to exercise regularly.

"How old was he when he died?" David asked.

"Eighty-eight."

"Then stop worrying about the matter," David said, laughing.

While dressing, I realized that Father's exercise routine mattered not a whit. There could be no genetic influence, for I was an adopted child, and this exchange in the doctor's office merely added another episode to a long history of meaningless opinions concerning my health and well being based on an assumed family heritage.

When I was around nine or ten, I would look in a mirror and ask myself questions about my appearance. What caused my nose to be precisely that shape? Why were my ears as flat against my skull as they were?

Where did my blue eyes come from? I remember that about that time I noticed that my sternum projected noticeably beyond what I thought it should. Greatly troubled by this phenomenon, I asked myself where it could possibly have originated. Even though in time this protuberance gradually disappeared, it was embarrassingly prominent in those days, and in my own childish way, I worried about it. Was it hereditary? Did it bode some strange medical misfortune? By the time I approached adolescence I had also discovered, much to my chagrin, that I suffered from a distinct lack of athletic prowess. Maybe, I thought, this unfortunate lack could be attributed to a kind of body imbalance, highlighted, all too clearly, by this protrusion. Where did it come from? Such questions troubled me more than I cared to admit. Perhaps they would be answered by my parents in due course. My parents had told me of my adoption several years earlier, but neither my parents nor I could conclusively answer these burning questions.

I can't remember precisely when Mother described my exact status, but it must have been very early in my life. Both Father and Mother believed in making my status perfectly clear and natural to me, and never during those formative years did this fact create anxiety. They pointed out, as soon as I was able to understand, that my mother was unable to have children, and they often exclaimed about how wonderful a day it had been when I came to live with them. At last they had someone upon whom they could lavish their love, to whom they could give devotion. The process of learning my adoptive state was so natural that I had little difficulty in sharing it, even with my classmates on the school playground. Instead of teasing me about my being adopted, my playmates let the matter drop, and I never felt odd or unaccepted. I recently mentioned this to a former classmate who confirmed my memory.

"Corky," she said, calling me by my childhood nickname, "we sure knew about it, but we never thought of you as anything but a Carson."

For years I relished my secret amusement when someone would tell Mother how much I resembled her physically in this or that way.

Mother never corrected the person but politely accepted the compliment, while inwardly I smiled.

*   *   *

I was born in Colorado and adopted by Charles and May Carson when I was four months old. My father was a pastor within a conservative Presbyterian denomination. At the time he was serving a congregation in Greeley, Colorado, but within a year following my adoption, we moved to central Kansas, where he took a teaching position at Sterling College, a small United Presbyterian institution. In this Kansas environment I spent my childhood; there I learned of my adoption and asked those questions before the mirror. Mother knew nothing about my life before the July day when I came to live with them except the date and place of my birth and my original given name. Her honesty led her to share this information with me during those early years, and I never forgot the name that she relayed to me—Jack Walsh. Even though it seemed to me odd to name a baby Jack rather than John, I would tell myself that Jack was a sturdy, no-nonsense name, typical of the kind of men who scouted the Rocky Mountains or panned for gold or mined silver. And I wondered if I came from such stock. It wasn't that I stored the name in my memory and toyed with it. The name lay dormant in my mind for years, yet I never forgot it, and eventually it became a key factor in my discovering my true identity. Whatever else I might fancy it to mean, the name indicated that my national origins were similar to those of my adoptive parents. I occasionally wondered how Mother had come to know the name when she knew nothing else. In this connection, she often mentioned her family physician, and I assumed that in some way it was he who arranged the adoption. She also made it clear to me early on that I had been a sickly child. Apparently, I had given both my parents many a sleepless night, for I suffered from colic.

Looking back now on those Kansas years of the 1920s and 30s, I discover that my dominant memories all have to do with contentment. The obvious love showered upon me by my parents contributed to this contentment. Mother kept a large, green baby book with a heavy, sturdy binding, filled with photographs and thoughts about me as well as the pertinent facts about my development. She often wrote in her clear hand about how blessed she felt herself to be, how precious I was to her and to Father, and with what wonder and joy they both watched as their "sweetest little feller" grew through infancy to boyhood.

She writes of celebrating that particular 4th of July when I arrived and of my appearance: "Very tiny and thin but oh those big blue eyes and the 'million dollar' smile!" She comments on the following page that not much else is to be said "but we fond parents see the 'angel in the block of marble.'" She notes my enjoyment of my bath and my "charming little giggle" but adds, "After he is in bed and lights are out, the giggle changes and we have an exhibition of Irish temper." Was this an assumption on her part, or did she know more than she ever revealed to me? Of course, she may have conjectured my supposed ethnic background from my name. Whatever the reason, I now know the statement to be at least partly correct.

Now that Father and Mother have died, I have often looked at that book. Beginning with the heavily decorated baptismal certificate, all the obligatory snapshots are there: baby boy in the perambulator; baby, wrapped up against the Colorado winter, smiling upon command for some doting relative or parishioner; the toddler holding on to the hand of an aunt or uncle; little boy in a Christopher Robin hat, learning to ride his first tricycle; father and son crouching above the oversize 1930 football helmet; Father, with his shock of dark hair and his black-rimmed glasses, holding his Bible against his vest, standing next to me; little guy with fond family members on an outing in the Rockies, where we spent our annual summer vacation.

As I discovered my adoptive status in those early years, I also saw how frail Mother appeared. A farm girl from southern Illinois, she had been orphaned at an early age and reared by numerous relatives, principally her maternal grandmother Matthews and her father's sister, Adaline, a generous, warm-hearted spinster. There were several Reformed Presbyterian churches in the area; she attended a country church near Sparta and Father another R. P. church in the next county. Both of them participated in the young people's activities shared by their respective churches and had plenty of opportunities to meet; both attended Sparta High School where acquaintance presumably blossomed into love. Their romance was one fact never shared with me. Father told me that he courted Mother for seven years during which time he had matriculated at Geneva College, the Reformed Presbyterian college located in Beaver Falls, Pennsylvania. From Father's freshman year at Geneva until he graduated from theological seminary, Father's devotion never wavered, nor did he ever assume that she could be his until he was fully prepared to support her.

Father entered college late because he was needed on the farm. Although Mother was five years his junior, she also attended Geneva one year behind him. Her finances were little better than his, and after two years of college she returned to Illinois and began to teach in a little country school near Rockford. Sometime during that period she suffered a serious illness that left her so emaciated that, according to Father's account, he scarcely recognized her upon his coming home from the seminary. Mother never shared with me the precise details of her illness, but I assumed that she had contracted the influenza during the great epidemic of 1917. Early on, I also learned that, presumably because of the influenza, Mother could never have children of her own, hence my coming into the family.

Because of her physical frailty, Mother suffered during her years in Kansas, but she seldom complained. The spring and summer would be especially difficult, for in the spring came the great dust storms that ravaged the land during the early 1930s. No matter how hard my parents tried to seal out the dust from the interior of the house, it managed to seep in at every window and door, sometimes leaving a quarter-inch-thick layer on the window sills. Mother would continually wipe away the dust, only to find it replaced within hours by another layer. The searing heat of summer would then bear down upon us, driven incessantly by the south wind leaving Mother prostrate. During those hot summers we often experienced spectacular thunderstorms that frightened both Mother and me. Although I never experienced a tornado, I do remember that the minute a thunderstorm approached from the west, Mother and I would scurry to the basement and wait it out in terror. We would watch the storm through the ground-level basement windows and witness the astonishing balls of fire hurling themselves past the windows at the precise moment we experienced the deafening clap of thunder. Sometimes a ball of fire would even hurl itself across our catacomb. Miraculously, we were never touched.

For Mother, there was no relief from the searing heat. In those dust bowl days the heat of summer would reach 100 degrees or more for days at a time. We had only small electric fans to cool ourselves. Nighttime offered little relief; we often went to the back yard, set up makeshift sleeping arrangements on the parched Bermuda grass and tried to sleep. But sleep seemed impossible for Mother, and gradually, as the summer wore on, she would find herself less and less able to function normally. By then Father was pastor of the local church, so when Father's month-long vacation arrived, we escaped to the Rockies, four hundred miles to the west.

*   *   *

I credit my happy sense of contentment to the attitude displayed by my adoptive parents in the face of these difficulties. Father, who could endure the Kansas summer without complaint, was obviously sensitive to Mother's condition. Even as a child, I sensed his deep concern. As I think back to those days, I realize how shocked and troubled he must have been to find the sweetheart he had left behind in Illinois so greatly changed physically and how troubled to realize that he and Mother could never have children of their own. His love for her remained and his fidelity was unquestionable. He had been used to disappointment, as evidenced by his late start in college. But Father had an unusual spirit. I seldom saw him visibly frustrated or upset about any matter. His was an unruffled spirit, and, though he had strong convictions, for the most part he avoided confrontation, even to the point where others took advantage of him on occasion. Many years later one of his former students told me how popular a teacher Father had been. Sometime during the 1928-29 academic year, however, the college administration informed him that they were not renewing his contract for the following year. When this decision became common knowledge, those of his students who were members of the Sterling Reformed Presbyterian congregation persuaded him to candidate for the then vacant pastorate. Ultimately, these students did not lose their teacher, for the congregation called him to be their pastor. He served the congregation until 1938 when, thanks to a new administration, he returned to a full-time teaching position at the college.

My father acquitted himself well in such situations, for he had a modest view of his own person and an often self-deprecating sense of humor. I remember one such incident occurring during the normally serious time of family devotions. It was Father's custom to conduct these devotions following the evening meal. He would read a passage from the Bible and close with a prayer. During that particular supper he and Mother had engaged in a lively discussion about the merits of Shakespeare; Mother defending the Bard vigorously and Father declaring his annoyance with Shakespeare's obscurity, an attitude on Father's part which surprised me. He freely admitted, however, that this position might have arisen from his own deficiency. The argument continued to the end of the meal. When Father opened his Bible to the passage for that evening, he read from Psalm 131, verse 1: "Lord, my heart is not haughty, nor mine eyes lofty: neither do I exercise myself in great matters, or in things too high for me." He never got beyond the first verse; instead, he broke into laughter, and our devotional time ended abruptly. This sense of humor carried Father through many a distressing situation.

Both he and Mother shared in my discipline, although my memories of such matters center more on Mother's sternness than on Father's. However, he left no doubt in my mind nor on my backside that his was a spare-the-rod-spoil-the-child philosophy. The Irish temper referred to by Mother in my baby scrapbook became a more serious problem as I grew older, and often I would openly defy my parents when they denied some request of mine. Having gotten my way in most instances, I would pout or throw a tantrum. The resulting spanking was inevitable. Punishment was brief; never did it involve a strap, although Mother, being less sturdy than Father, sometimes employed a switch gathered from a handy bush and stripped of its leaves. My parents were, however, judicious in their discipline. I remember a particular incident from my high school days that must have greatly embarrassed my parents. As a member of the band, I was participating in a Fourth of July celebration in Lyons, the county seat. The band drove there in autos volunteered by supportive parents. I rode on this particular occasion in the automobile of Cecil Crawford, the band director. I carried with me a small packet of firecrackers and some matches. After we arrived in Lyons my enthusiasm led me to toss the lighted firecrackers out the window, all the while striking my matches on the outside of Mr. Crawford's car door, ruining the paint. This act of stupidity eventually led to Father's paying for the damage, yet there was no spanking. Perhaps I had grown too big. I think, however, that Father knew that a stern rebuke was sufficient. My acute embarrassment had been punishment enough. Father was never cruel, for love tempered his sometimes painful administration of discipline.

As I grew older I sensed some of my parents' particular bogeymen, John Dewey, with his theories of progressive education, being one. My father's brother, Roy, was in those days a member of a progressive clique at Greeley State Teachers College in Colorado where he served as Registrar, and

Father and he spent many hours discussing the merits of their respective positions on educational theory. Father had retained much of his down-to-earth, biblically oriented views on the role of parents in education and the use of discipline in the public schools, and, even though Uncle Roy remained in the conservative church of his youth, he vigorously defended Dewey's educational theories.

Educational theories, however, were not blazing topics of discussion at Sterling College. Father's studies in sociology and economics at Greeley State had eventually led him to take his family to Kansas. Sterling College, like the community around it, was conservative, so that a virtual unanimity of views precluded argument, even as an intellectual exercise. I found myself, then, growing up in an atmosphere where conservatism dictated the social mores: in religion, Protestant; in politics, Republican. Ethnically, the community was predominately white and Anglo-Saxon. I cannot remember knowing a single Jew, Italian or Eastern European before I left Sterling. The old home town sported exactly one Roman Catholic family who traveled to Lyons, ten miles to the north, to attend mass. A daughter was my classmate, and the class considered her to be simply a curiosity—an anomaly.

Discrimination did occur in this small, Midwestern town, but it failed to impinge on my childhood consciousness. Several African-American families lived among us, and, though I knew that they lived in a particular section of the town, I did not see that fact as segregation. Among this number were the Rawlins, Kern and Grissom families. Ardis Rawlins, a classmate, never struck me as being unusual except in color. Again, there seemed to be no clearly overt discriminatory acts taken by either teachers or students. I remember Father, however, seemingly unaware of the implications of his actions, often regaling his family and friends by reproducing down to the very accents the jokes found on a scratchy phonograph record that we possessed entitled "The Two Black Crows." Nor did we give special thought to the fact that one of our favorite radio programs that we listened to regularly and happily was

Amos and Andy. Ben Rawlins, a respected laborer at the local grain elevator, had five sons who had gained a certain fame by means of their superior athletic ability. Despite this fact, they were apparently fully aware of their status. No African-American lived north of the railroad tracks. Most Sterling residents subtly considered the south end of town, across the tracks, as a somewhat run down area, not quite equal to the remaining residential areas even though the majority of citizens there were white. Once, Father recounted at the supper table a conversation he had had with one of the Rawlins boys at the college that day following the sociology class. The discussion was pleasant enough, for Father was seldom argumentative. As "Dukes" turned to leave my father, he smiled: "Someday," he said, "we folks is goin' to get you folks." I could sense that Father was troubled by the remark, but we never discussed it further. Forty years later, I discovered, much to my surprise, that the Sterling cemetery, an almost perfectly square section of land at the north end of town, had a small but distinct corner, reserved exclusively for African-Americans, a mirror image of the corner of town where they lived. Segregation even to the grave.

Republicanism was so strong in the area that Democrats achieved a notoriety of sorts by their very existence. Many years after leaving Sterling I learned that in 1872 a group of settlers from the East had migrated to this locale. They were Congregationalists who established a church in town that continued to exist for some time. Gradually, however, they left that communion and joined the other local churches or departed the Faith altogether. Many of these citizens stood, both religiously and politically, to the left of everyone else in the region. Inevitably, they were Democrats—and suspect. Among the most vocal was one unmarried woman. Georgia Pence shocked the community with regularity, professing herself to be a free-thinker, a supporter of every cause considered by the good people of the community as anathema, for free thinking in Sterling was tantamount to atheism. The autumn of 1932, then, became a traumatic time for many, including my parents.

My favorite ball field, a property of the school district, was close to our house. As I played softball or touch football that summer and fall on the playground, I became increasingly aware that something important was occurring. It was, in fact, a political campaign, the first that I had ever been aware of. One September afternoon, I was awaiting my turn at bat. As I stood there, I heard the sound of music far to the south. By the time I had struck out and seated myself dejectedly on the bench, the blare of music was upon us. Creeping slowly along the dirt street behind us, loud-speakers mounted at the front and rear, came a Model A Ford pickup truck. The noise was deafening; the music upbeat. I turned to see the source. Horror of horrors! We had been invaded by the Democrat Party. Whether we wished it or not, "Happy Days" were here again. The truck slowly made its way to the corner, turned to the west and disappeared. The last thing to be seen was the picture of a jaunty Franklin Delano Roosevelt, promising this staunch Republican town—who knew what?

Here was another family anathema, a politician who dared to suggest the repeal of the 18th Amendment that had legalized the prohibition of alcoholic beverages in the United States. Mother, especially, had a difficult time with both of the Roosevelts, and I was thoroughly indoctrinated with the notion that the Democratic Party was to be equated with the wrong. Could there be a good Democrat? For most of us the question was simply rhetorical. After all, the town atheist was a Democrat. One of the prominent farmers who dared to cut his wheat on the Sabbath was a Democrat. Most of the townspeople who danced and played cards were at least suspected of being Democrats. A famous example of one who had fallen from grace was Doris Fleeson, a Sterling girl, who had become one of the leading liberal journalists in America. Other home town products, professors and poets, had apparently found the local atmosphere too stultifying and pursued their liberal ways else-where. There was, however, an intriguing exception. One member of our own congregation was a vocal Democrat. Ed Wilkey, a relatively prosperous wheat farmer, often argued with Father about the merits of this liberal party; rumor had it that Ed voted regularly in political elections, a practice then prohibited by our church's standards. He was simply the exception that proved the rule. Mother and Father never forgave F. D. R. for his treachery in bringing about Repeal; nothing Franklin did, nothing Eleanor espoused was ever granted unqualified approval. As I look back now on this period of my life, I realize how thoroughly my conservative religious and political views were being fused by my environment.

*   *   *

Sometime before we moved to Kansas my Great Aunt Addie had come to live with us. She was my initiation to the older generation. Adaline Finley was Mother's paternal aunt, a spinster who had reared my mother when she had been orphaned. She had cared for Mother in her home in Sparta until Mother had gone to college and secured a teaching position. Mother believed it to be her Christian duty to care for Aunt Addie in her old age. Aunt Addie was by then an elderly, wizened woman, with a little bun of hair on the top of her head and tiny, round wire-rimmed glasses. She wore her old-fashioned clothing with dignity, and, despite her obvious love for me, she failed to sublimate her stern demeanor, a product of her Victorian upbringing. From my perspective as a small child, the most remarkable fact about Aunt Addie was that she had been born in 1847, long before the Civil War. About the time I was seven, I applied what I had learned in arithmetic class and marveled that I was younger then than Aunt Addie had been when Booth assassinated President Lincoln! To me Aunt Addie represented a distant era, filled with mystery. I know now that she represented my sole intimate connection with the Victorian Age. I never came to know her frame of reference thoroughly, however, for Aunt Addie died when I was nine.

My Aunt Grace, however, was an entirely different matter. Mother's older sister represented a newer, more daring age. She too had never married, but for a small boy she carried with her the mysterious air of one who surely had been courted by some dashing suitor and who, for some reason best known to her, had rejected him. She was too pretty, too vivacious and too generous never to have been pursued by someone. Indeed, there were hints of romance, faint whispers echoing throughout the family conversations but never spoken aloud. My aunt, a regular visitor at the Christmas season, always brought a bounty of good gifts. Like her younger sister, she too adored this little lad who had come to the family. The gifts were not lavish, her income as a school teacher would not permit it, but what gifts they were! The most valuable, for their influence upon my formative years, were the books she regularly presented to me—tales of adventure, stories of the world of nature, Mother Goose, the books of A. A. Milne, Robert Louis Stevenson and Rudyard Kipling. And to visit her—that too was one of the highlights of each summer, for she also lived in Greeley and functioned as a sort of official welcoming committee to the Rocky Mountains that I soon learned to love.

By a quirk of circumstance Aunt Grace's maternal Aunt Eliza Elder, rather than Aunt Addie, had taken her in upon my grandparents' death; subsequently, she had become a member of a different conservative denomination, the United Presbyterian Church. As I grew older I discovered that my parents considered this denomination somewhat less strict than ours, less apt to hew to the traditional conservative line. As a result, there clung to Aunt Grace a faint air of adventure, although, in matters of personal belief, she differed little from Mother. She remained more than slightly glamorous to me, for she had gone to New Mexico to nurse the desperately ill during the influenza epidemic in 1917. Moreover, she played bridge! One close friend, her bridge partner, Mabel, fascinated me, for I remember her particularly as a bobbed, strawberry blonde who actually smoked cigarettes! I was certain that Aunt Grace was not so tainted, but the very fact that she could maintain a deep friendship with this woman intrigued me. Here was a woman who could, after all, maintain her religious convictions at the same time finding much to enjoy in the world outside the church.

*   *   *

My early religious training was intense and thorough. In my very early years, when Father was not pastoring a congregation, he continued to preach fairly regularly, supplying vacant pulpits in Kansas and Nebraska. I would often accompany him on these trips while Mother remained at home, especially if the weather were hot. My parents expected me to attend the church services on the Lord's Day, both morning and evening, and to show up regularly at the mid-week prayer meeting. Our conservative community, moreover, associated the word *Sunday* with the secular world, and eschewed this word in favor of *the Sabbath*. The vibrant fellowship of that small-town congregation, composed principally of wheat farmers and a sprinkling of teachers and other professionals, left an indelible mark on my life. After the congregation called Father to be their pastor, I soon learned what it meant to be the preacher's kid. It didn't take long for me to discover that the pastor and his family lived in a fishbowl. Every move was monitored; little escaped the eye of those who for reasons best known to themselves wished to embarrass any P. K. who attempted to practice what the church taught as exemplary virtues of the Christian life.

The congregation, however, was remarkably considerate. In those days Father's salary was minuscule at best, yet these dust bowl farmers, whose income scarcely allowed them the luxury of a security beyond the sunset of each day, lavished what they had in goods and services to augment Father's salary. There was a continual flow of farm produce arriving at our door: vegetables, milk, eggs, and a variety of flesh and fowl, enough to establish constant nourishment and a balanced diet. If these good people could not pay more than the minimum, they would certainly see to it that the preacher's family had the necessities for a comfortable life.

I was a skinny towhead blessed with a good mind, a retentive memory and a lively imagination rather than athletic ability. My awkwardness embarrassed, even humiliated me. In junior high I determined to go out for the basketball team, and, although my one shining moment came when I let fly a last-second, improbable, off-balance shot that won the game, I never repeated that performance, for this was also my last year of varsity basketball. Sterling High School had a well-respected athletic program and a coach who terrified me. Probably Harry Detter was no better nor worse than any of his fraternity, but for me he was a ferocious lion, king of the beasts! Only those whom he favored could possibly survive his sarcasm and anger. High school basketball was definitely not for me. A small coterie of athletes, usually older than I, saw to it that I was the butt of numerous insults. I had to prove to them that I could excel physically in some small way. I decided that the answer would be to try out for the track team.

Track was a big time athletic event in the Kansas high schools, and while I was too skinny to participate in the field events, perhaps I could run. Vernal Duncan was definitely a milder mannered coach than Coach Detter, and, I suspect, encouraged me to whatever level of competence he felt I could reach and then let me alone. So, for two torturous springs I ran. We practiced at the nearby college athletic field. The quarter-mile college track seemed endless. Even once around the perimeter brought on pain, perhaps only mental, but certainly related to the physical—side aches, burning lungs, rubbery legs that simply would not carry me to the finish line.

We would often run timed trials in the midst of the driving, burning spring winds that whipped up the dust storms. I marveled at my teammates who could speed around the track and seem scarcely winded. One year we had a new kid, a missionary's son named Alfred Heasty, a tall, gangly boy from the Sudan, who ran the distance races. He loped around the track effortlessly and seemed able to win almost at will. Much to my surprise and personal satisfaction, he was an active

Christian. Somehow, I had begun to equate my P.K. status with my natural athletic shortcomings, an assumption no doubt encouraged by my tormentors. Heasty proved to me otherwise, but I concluded, finally, that competitive athletics were not for me, and I took up activities more natural to my interests; I joined the chorus and the band and took up acting.

Music had always been a part of my life. Both Mother and Aunt Grace had sung to me for as long as I could remember. Father was a natural but untrained tenor, and he loved to sing as well. They introduced me to an extensive repertoire of nineteenth-century parlor songs and patriotic music from both the Civil War and World War I. The Reformed Presbyterian Church adhered to a strict policy of exclusive Psalm singing in worship, unaccompanied by any musical instrument; therefore, a cappella singing developed in me an early interest in vocal music, particularly in four-part harmony. The last thing one could have expected in a non-liturgical church such as ours would have been a boys choir, yet the precentor, a tall, rugged farmer blessed with a strong singing voice, recruited us boys at a tender age to sing with the women in the choir. When I was about ten I would sit with Mother in the hard pew almost directly in front of Father who occupied the pulpit and envy the young men and women who filled the choir loft immediately to Father's right. I longed for the day when I too would take my place in the choir. Eventually, that day came. At twelve I joined the church, and at the same time I joined the choir, even though I still sang soprano. Eventually, I learned to sing the appropriate part once my voice changed, first alto, then tenor. During these years, my love for music and for the church developed simultaneously.

In junior high and high school I assumed a modest role in the marching band, playing second trumpet. I was content to play a lesser role, although I sometimes dreamed of one day matching the skill of Robert Ashlock, the first chair trumpeter, effortlessly producing his soaring melodies and pure tone. My accomplishments in choir were more substantial. By my sophomore year in high school I had established myself as a reliable tenor, although on at least one occasion I proved to be a thorn in the flesh. Our director, a young, enthusiastic woman was leading us through the Stephen Foster favorite, "Jeanie with The Light Brown Hair." By then, my confidence as a tenor knew no bounds. The pretty young director knew exactly whom she could count on. I could even get away with a musical joke if I wished. We came to the appropriate passage. It was my chance to be cute. I sang as lustily as I could, "Borne like a heifer on the summer air." Miss Urquhart instantly rapped on her music stand, glared at me; then broke into tears. I was ordered to the principal's office in disgrace.

My love for the theater began in my sophomore year of high school. I discovered that when I entered into a role and became someone else, my shyness and lack of confidence disappeared. My first role was that of the romantic hero in the standard English thriller, "The Ghost Train" by Arnold Ridley. I must have been a callow romantic lead! At sixteen I still had never had so much as one date. So, when Miss Johnson, the drama teacher, instructed me to kiss my leading lady, my total inexperience collided with the excitement of anticipated pleasure. My classmate, Jo Ray, was, however, a good sport; she led the way and never once indicated that she might have been less than thrilled by my fumbling approach.

I found that my contentment, rooted in a happy home, was enhanced by my participation in those social activities where I could sense a measure of accomplishment without compromising my religious convictions.

*   *   *

From Mother and Father I also received other indelible influences. From my mother, particularly, came my initial introduction to literature. Aunt Grace supplied many of the books, but it was Mother who read to me, fostering my literary interests in later years. Mother's taste in literature was remarkably broad given her limited rural background and brief college career. By the time she had finished her sophomore year in college and had begun her teaching, she had developed a love for what one usually calls classic literature, and even fifty years later, as I prepared to teach a Shakespeare play or a Dickens novel, I could hear Mother's peculiar use of an apt phrase: "sweets to the sweet," upon offering me a bit of candy; "good night sweet prince," when tucking me into bed; "something will turn up," when I was filled with childish frustration by the failure of anticipated pleasure.

From my father I inherited my love for sports; this intense interest, combined with my less than spectacular prowess, created my frustration whenever I attempted to compete. Father introduced me to competitive athletics as a spectator, for he was, throughout his teaching career at the college, the Athletic Director. In this role he had close contact with the athletes, and this enabled me to spend much of my spare time on the athletic fields or in the gymnasium, so I easily caught his enthusiasm for sports.

Father never lost his deep affection for the traditions of the farming community. Having been reared on a small farm in Southern Illinois— "little Egypt" as it was called—he cultivated his farming roots, despite his receiving a college education and permanently leaving the farm. We always attempted a vegetable garden, even in the worst of the dust bowl years. Mother played her part as well, attempting, sometimes fruitlessly, to grow a few flowers. To this day I find little enjoyment in cultivating those rare flowers hardy enough to withstand a burning Kansas summer—zinnias and hollyhocks among the more memorable. Father, a model pastor, was always willing to go into the fields to help a farmer who might need assistance in an emergency, often during the wheat harvest working the combine when necessary.

While his taste in music was not nearly so catholic as my mother's was in literature, he loved to sing, his tenor providing a constant musical ambiance around the house. Whenever we traveled in the automobile, we three would sing together: "Tenting Tonight on the Old Campground,"

"Marching Through Georgia," "Silver Threads Among the Gold," "It's a Long Way to Tipperary," and "Pack Up Your Troubles." Father broadened the repertoire with a lengthy version of "Mr. Gallagher and Mr. Shean." I am certain that Father never dreamed that this popular patter song came from the Ziegfeld Follies. No matter. Travel with my parents was always fun.

*   *   *

For all but the earliest years of my childhood I lived directly across from the college campus. As campuses go, Sterling's was not especially grand, but it was large enough to provide an imaginative youngster a wide range of activities. Being an only child, I found myself inventing an imaginary playmate named Bob who would accompany me and my live mongrel terrier, Tippy, across the state highway from my house to the campus where we would roam and play at our pleasure throughout much of the spring and on into autumn. Directly across the highway from the manse was possibly the one outstanding feature of the campus, the Sunken Garden, an artificial declivity perhaps eighty by twenty yards. In the exact center stood a small round fishpond with a two-foot high, rough cement wall, stocked with a few tiny goldfish and fed by a small fountain. On its upper perimeter a privet hedge protected the garden from invaders. One might expect flowers to fill such a garden, but Kansas summers precluded that happy condition. My chief memory is that the only touch of color there was provided by the red and yellow cannas growing within the garden confines. There were also two impressive clumps of pampas grass located on either side of the fishpond, half the distance to the end of the garden. Despite the scarcity of flowers, the garden provided me with an excellent expanse of grass in which to carry out my private adventures—sweating though the African savannas on our safaris or storming the nearest slope topped by its protective wall to capture the enemy fortress or tumbling down the banks in momentary retreat. On the campus there was simply no other bank which one could roll down, for the campus was as perfectly flat as everywhere else in my hometown.

Because there existed an underground river six feet beneath the town, flowing parallel with the nearby Arkansas River (the local pronunciation Ar—Kansas), the college was favored with an endless supply of water; consequently, the campus gave the appearance in those days of an oasis. The Bermuda and bluegrass lawn was watered by means of long one-inch galvanized pipes lying on the surface of the ground. There were small, hexagonal jets located at regular intervals along the pipe. When the scheduled watering took place, a continuous spray enveloped great sections of the campus; I found the walls of spray extending across the campus a perfect way to beat the heat. When occasionally a tiny orifice would become plugged with debris, I acted as a self-appointed maintenance man, carrying with me a stiff piece of grass that I would insert into the hole to release the water again.

The underlying river provided another grand summer escape for me and my friends. We would gather in Father's garden behind the manse armed with shovels, and, digging industriously in what had once passed for a potato patch, we would excavate a cave, in reality a hole remarkably similar to a grave, large enough for two or three of us to hide in. We were never able to dig below six feet, for at that depth we would strike a mixture of sand and coarser gravel, smooth pearls of rock that we treasured. To dig deeper was folly, for inevitably water began to seep into the bottom of the pit. We secured an abandoned door to cover the hole and, having invited a couple of other neighborhood children, we engaged in battle, the pit being our trench. Three warriors crouched in the trench; three besieged us from the garden with convenient clods recently turned up by Father. The warfare was usually harmless enough, but it got out of hand once when, running low on clods, the attackers filled tin cans with earth. One can crashed through a rotten portion of the door and struck me directly on top of my head. We arranged a hasty truce, and I appeared before my astonished mother, bloody but unbowed, the blood trickling down my face. It must have been a gruesome sight. Mother rushed me to the doctor's office where Dr. Trueheart stitched me properly. The truce became an armistice; war games were henceforth prohibited. Eventually, the pit took on water and collapsed.

Swimming was not a part of my childhood days in Sterling, even though there was a swimming pool located next to the icehouse at the far end of town. Mother somehow had received the impression that the pool was unclean; she discouraged me from swimming there, and I had to settle for an occasional foray into the Arkansas River itself, for there were spots here and there where the channel might run as much as six feet deep, so I could get at least a taste of what it meant to swim. My friends and I spent many summer afternoons on the sandbars, damming up the rivulets, redirecting them to suit our fancy, wading along cool stretches underneath the tall cottonwoods, watching the cotton blowing in the wind, swinging from a rope tied to a branch directly above a large pool and plunging into the pool amid shouts of joy as our bodies struck the water. We tried, unsuccessfully, to catch with our bare hands the few fish we encountered, and we would return to the town, gloriously happy, plotting to resume our river adventures at the earliest convenience. During my adolescence the town fathers developed a small sandpit located at the south end of town into Sterling Lake, with picnic facilities and a bathhouse. Some years later the lake gained a small share of fame as one of the locations for the movie *Picnic*. The swimming pool and icehouse disappeared.

Still, the campus was my favorite childhood domain, and I could roam it at will, returning after supper on long summer evenings to play until the darkness began to descend, and the four-o-clocks alongside Wilson Gymnasium, shimmering with the visiting Sphinx moths, filled the dusk with their heavy, sweet fragrance.

*   *   *

The church was, in great measure, the center of my Kansas child-hood. We worshipped in a large, white frame building two blocks south of the manse. Architecturally, the church was unimpressive. It was an ungainly structure occupying the corner of the block. Its builders, no doubt influenced by a traditional desire for plainness, had deliberately omitted a spire. Nothing gothic for them. The large basement housed the kitchen and the Church School rooms. The sanctuary, occupying the upper level of the building, was reached by two sets of stairs, effectively creating a difficult ascent for the elderly faithful. The room was large, the pews ranged in a semi-circle in front of the platform and choir loft. The congregation met for its midweek prayer meeting in a smaller room at the rear, usually closed off from the sanctuary but opened for the semi-annual communion service. As a young boy, not yet a member of the congregation, I can remember sitting alone in our pew watching, as my mother and other members of the congregation solemnly made their way to the communion tables in the smaller room. As they went they would sing the question from Psalm 24: "Who is the man who shall ascend into the hill of God?" Within a few years, I had joined the procession and was responding in song with the answer: "Whose hands are pure; whose heart is clean, And unto vanity, / Who has not lifted up his soul nor sworn deceitfully." A terribly sobering assertion for a young teenager. The congregation would seat themselves at the long, narrow tables, covered with white linen, there to partake of the bread and the grape juice (wine was strictly forbidden). Following the celebration the congregation solemnly returned once more from the small room to their pews. A balcony, filled only at very large funerals, occupied the space above this room. The worship service was invariably unadorned and solemn, but it was accompanied by one unique feature. During the service the entire congregation often experienced a faint but noticeable earth tremor. This phenomenon came not from the religious enthusiasm of the congregation, nor from the preacher's pulpit pounding (Father was a quiet preacher), nor from the Lord on high, but from the building standing next to the church. The waterworks housed several DeLaval turbine pumps. These giant engines, a constant source of fascination to the town's children, drew the town's water supply from the underground river and, at the same time, generated the town's electricity. Although they operated quietly for the most part, the engines often shook the entire block, producing the Sabbath trembling, so puzzling to any stranger in our midst.

As in most rural communities of that era, our social life as well as our spiritual life centered in the church. There were, of course, the church dinners, with their abundant variety of food, served in the cool, somewhat musty basement. In the Sterling congregation there were at least two large, extended families, to whose annual picnics on such holidays as Memorial Day and the Fourth of July the pastor's family was always invited, for we had no immediate relatives in the congregation. These gatherings were alive with the activity of games—a variety of races, dodge ball, capture the flag, volleyball. The social activities extended throughout the year. In Kansas, November was often so warm that on Thanksgiving Day when these large families held one of their feasts, we children, dressed as if for summer, played our annual game of touch football out of doors, moving indoors only to eat.

*   *   *

One annual event gave me supreme joy. I looked forward to our annual trek to Colorado that took place each summer during Father's four-week vacation that provided our necessary escape from the Kansas heat. We would pack up the car and head for the Colorado Rockies at night, arising, sometimes as early as three in the morning, and driving at the thrilling speed of 40 miles per hour in our 1926 Model T Ford or our 1930 Wyllis Whippet across the plains. We drove through the parched towns in the western counties, imperceptibly climbing in elevation until we finally reached the buttes and arroyos of eastern Colorado. Here we would invariably play the "who can see them first" game, "them" being the Front Range of the Rockies. We strained our eyes unnecessarily, long before we caught a glimpse of the peaks, but one of us would suddenly cry out, "There they are!" For by then we could see, far ahead, the low-lying, purple saw teeth of the Rockies, rising just above the western horizon, often overtopped by a layer of dark cloud. The confirmation of the mountain's presence, caused us to imagine a distinct cooling effect, even though the temperature remained above one hundred degrees. Gradually, inevitably, the purple mountain range would grow slowly along the horizon, and soon we could identify the individual peaks: Pike's Peak far to the south, a lonely sentinel, standing out from the range, or Long's Peak to the north, with its square head, the magnet around which centered every happy anticipation of the cool pleasure to come.

Father had once owned a small cabin in Glen Haven, Colorado, along the North Fork of the Big Thompson River near Rocky Mountain National Park but in a rash moment had sold it when he moved to Kansas. The cabin's new owner belonged to the Greeley congregation, and he made it our privilege to stay there for at least a portion of our vacation. For me, these days in the mountains were the highlight of each year. Uncle Roy Carson's four children provided abundant companionship for an only child. During these summer visits we roamed throughout Greeley from the beacon tower atop Inspiration Point on the south to Island Grove Park on the north. We bicycled along the wide streets lined with (for a Kansas boy) incredibly large elms towering over lush, perfectly manicured lawns, kept so by the strictly regulated sprinkling schedule.

In the mountains themselves, hiking along the trails occupied much of our time. We would hike to the Lost Village, far beyond the end of our road, or to Fern Lake, Alberta Falls, Hallet's Peak, or Andrews Glacier along the Front Range in Rocky Mountain National Park. When the plan for the day did not call for a hike, we invariably went stream fishing. Nothing fancy for us, no modern gear, no hand-tied flies, but worms dug up the night before and now encased in the flat

Prince Albert tobacco can carried in the rear pocket of our khaki work pants. We moved across the slippery logs and over the boulders, sometimes on a trail well worn by the fishermen who had gone before us, sometimes through the alder thickets, the nettles and the clusters of columbines to our favorite spots, those deep, quiet pools just beneath the falls or cascades where we knew for certain the big ones lay. All sense of time lost, we worked our way upstream for hours, pausing briefly for sandwiches when we could no longer ignore our hunger. We drank directly from the stream, for in those days one considered none but the smallest stream dangerous to one's health. Nearly every afternoon the rains came, the storm, brief and heavy, accompanied by a few moments of impressive lightning and thunder when we would duck under an overhanging rock to keep dry. So with creels filled with our limit of fern-wrapped trout, we would make our way back, much more rapidly this time, knowing that the premature darkness of the mountain canyon would soon overtake us. In the evening, after a supper of trout, often accompanied by some wild concoction prepared by Father, we gathered before the fireplace, watching the dancing flames and planning our next day's activities, or we huddled about the cleared table, a Coleman lantern or a kerosene lamp illuminating the game we were engrossed in and providing all the heat necessary for us to soften our Black Cow candy stick on which we chewed with relish. The game completed, we laughed at our sick jokes and, making a sometimes ineffective attempt to establish a reverent mood, we allowed Father to conduct family prayers before we climbed into bed, lulled into a deep sleep by the roar of the mountain stream just beyond the cabin walls.

Greeley was the home of other family members besides Uncle Roy. Aunt Grace taught in the Cameron elementary school and lived across from the college campus. There were distant cousins of Mother's who lived in nearby La Salle. Several family members from an earlier generation had migrated from Southern Illinois, beginning shortly after the Civil War. The family who provided my boyhood with some of its most delightful experiences was the Faris family who lived on a farm northeast of the city. Here I came to understand the joys and sorrows of the farmer who lived by irrigation. Mother's cousin, Finley Faris, grew sugar beets, alfalfa, and potatoes. The prosperity of the farm rose or fell with the vagaries of the preceding winter's snowfall. When the reservoirs, dotting the landscape along the foot of the Front Range, were full, prospects were high; when the runoff was low, dire consequences almost certainly ensued. Even when expectations seemed certain, disaster, in the form of a slashing hailstorm, could ruin the crops. As a small child, I was scarcely aware of these trials, and for the most part spent my time romping about the farm, BB gun in hand, shooting "spatchies," as the English Sparrows were called, roistering with Rover, the family collie, going barefoot while trying to avoid the Mexican sandburrs which flourished everywhere, and accompanying Cousin Finley as he walked the ditch, shovel in hand, and turned the water into the beet rows. I would entertain myself for hours in the concrete-block bunkhouse behind the house or explore the underground tornado cellar filled with sacks of potatoes. I especially enjoyed tagging along behind Cousin Finley's two daughters, Betty and Barbara, when they were sent to pick up the mail at the crossroads where the Mexican farm laborer's house stood. I was fascinated when allowed to accompany my cousins as they delivered eggs to the Mexicans. It was my first cross-cultural experience, exciting but essentially meaningless to me.

So it was that during these childhood years I developed a deep and abiding love for my adoptive family, who had welcomed and unconditionally loved me. They *were* my family; I knew no other, nor did I show any interest in discovering who my birth family might be. The roots of both Father's and Mother's families lay in the region southeast of St. Louis, and before that in Ulster, far away across the sea. The Carsons had emigrated in the 1840s from County Monaghan, the Finleys twenty years earlier, from County Antrim. Some of the Carsons had come directly to Illinois; others through Pennsylvania; the Finleys came by way of South Carolina, where they lived until faced with the ultimate question of slave ownership, at which time they elected to migrate northward. My interest in family and roots began in those early years, particularly when I would visit my paternal grandparents in Southern Illinois or my cousins in Colorado. I was a comfortable Scotch-Irish lad, and through this period I developed a strong sense of identity. I had a heritage, both ethnic and religious, conservative and Protestant, undoubtedly the reason that, for many years, I never voiced, even inwardly, the question of my true roots, my blood heritage. I was, in virtually every sense of the phrase, a contented child.

Grace Finley, Norman, 1925

Norman, 1930
Sterling, Kansas

Adaline Finley, Norman, 1927
Sterling College

Charles Carson, Norman, 1928
Sterling

Norman Carson, 1935

Samuel Wells II, 1949

William C. Hurt, Maude Lee Hurt
c. 1885

William Rhodes, Ida Rhodes
c.1910

Edna Rhodes
c.1918

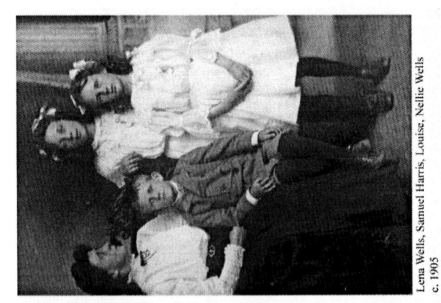

Lena Wells, Samuel Harris, Louise, Nellie Wells
c. 1905

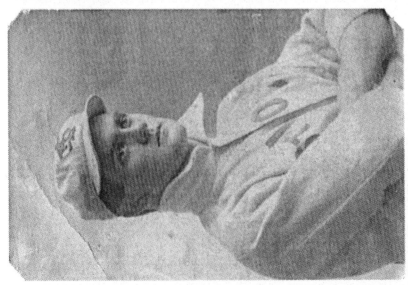

Charles "Dusty" Rhodes
c. 1909

Wells house, 921 Lincoln Avenue, Las Vegas, N.M.
1896

Hurt house, 910 Jackson Avenue, Las Vegas, N.M., 1988

2

Am I My Brother's Finder?

That visit to my internist made it apparent that I had a serious problem concerning my annual physical. I was reluctant to admit it, but there it was! As I sat in the doctor's office, I began to fill out the obligatory forms. Weight, probably too heavy; height, had I begun to shrink? Most older people do. Well, I would pretend anyway that I had not. Color of eyes, still the same old blue although my spectacles had for years partially obscured that fact. Color of hair, ah, there was a change. Where had the little towhead gone? "Blond" still fit the bill but not very convincingly. How about "dirty blond"? I decided that in this instance the pejorative was gratuitous. Father's and mother's names, I never gave it a thought. Living or dead, both were now gone, having lived good and rich lives into their eighties. Cause of father's death, natural causes, as far as could be determined. Then the same old problem arose. At the point of answering the next question, cause of mother's death, I glanced down the sheet to the succeeding inquiries and realized why I was being asked these particular questions, for a series of questions followed which clearly depended upon the relationship of their deaths to the medical and genetic inheritance I would have received from them. Nothing about the death or medical history of either Mother or Father Carson could make the slightest difference in my case. There was no true biological medical history. Nothing that I might enter about my adoptive parents would mean anything to the physician. For I had no genetic information to offer, no genetic history whatsoever!

We had moved from Kansas to Western Pennsylvania when I was a junior in high school. My contentment as an adopted child was so thorough that, throughout the sixteen years I lived in Kansas, the final years of high school and my four years at Geneva College in Pennsylvania, I never gave my adopted status a second thought, except when it became necessary to inform some curious friend about it. I would describe my status in the most matter-of-fact terms, and if asked whether I was curious about my forbears, I could honestly claim not to be.

As I now reflect on this lack of curiosity, several reasons for my attitude become apparent. I had developed a sense of self-assurance rooted in the strong familial ties established by my adoptive parents and by both sides of my extended family. Never did I feel resentful about my birth mother's putting me up for adoption. To me my adoptive mother and father *were* my mother and father, and I accepted this fact as a part of God's divine plan for my life. Undergirding this attitude was the security provided by the religious heritage and training given me by my parents. Unlike many who have grown up within strict religious conservatism, I seldom had doubts about the fundamental truths of the Christian Faith. The teasing that I often received because I was a "preacher's kid," usually hardened rather than weakened my conservative stance.

Furthermore, as nearly as I can remember, my teachers delighted in me, for I found almost every area of my schooling interesting. Many years later one of my elementary school classmates, never noted for his academic enthusiasm, confided that his clearest memory of me was that I was a "walking encyclopedia," often the source of necessary information but probably, for others, more than a little frustration as well. Gradually, I had overcome my embarrassment at being less than athletically adept and had for that weakness substituted my academic abilities. It took many years for me to realize that not only had I developed a protective shell in this way but also a somewhat irritating egotism as well. Because of the early instances of torment suffered at the hands of my athletic schoolmates, I developed a scorn for almost all athletes (save those who were my special friends) that, paradoxically, warred against my avid interest in sports. By the time I entered college, however, I was able to reconcile this dichotomy and live self-confidently with my received identity.

Furthermore, throughout my childhood an acceptance of one's adoptive status was much more likely to be taken for granted than it has become in recent years. I knew few other adoptees, but they seemed no more curious to find their roots than I. One reason for the change in attitude that has taken place over the years is undoubtedly the amount of media publicity given to such matters. The number of children need-ing to be adopted has increased, and there appear to be many more pressing circumstances, both positive and negative, surrounding adoptees desiring to find their birth parents. The media take great interest in long-lost children finding their siblings in happy circum-stances. There are, however, horror stories as well. Throughout my early life I seldom heard of such cases. Consequently, I was never especially curious about my status.

A third reason for my never having searched out my roots is that until quite recently almost all the states had strict confidentiality laws that dis-couraged adoptees from seeking out their birth family. Many still do. I had never confronted such laws, but occasionally, such information had drifted my way. I had little interest in mounting such a legal challenge.

Essentially, however, my lack of interest grew out of the feeling of secu-rity generated by my adoptive parents. The sorts of questions that I have described persisted—why was I blue-eyed, where did my prominent ster-num come from, why did I become nearsighted by the time I was sixteen, where did my short fuse temper originate (both Mother and Father were unusually calm persons)? There seemed to be no easy answers for these questions. The answer, I assumed, lay in my genetic background; yet I never pursued it. My interest in music, however, seemed to come from my environment, particularly from my family and church. My intelligence I attributed to God, but I also recognized the inevitable genetic source. Still, I usually credited my upbringing for my developing interest in the world in which I lived, particularly in science and literature.

I developed, for example, an interest in history that soon became centered in genealogy but not the genealogy of my biological family. Instead, I found myself more and more interested in the roots of my adoptive family. I identified so closely with them that I began to search out the forbears of both Father's and Mother's families. As an adult I eventually had the opportunity to live in Northern Ireland for a year, and I spent much time tracing the paternal and maternal sides of both my adoptive parents, for all four of these families were from Ulster. I accepted as *mine* the Carson, Finley, Moffett, Ramsey, Matthews and Campbell roots. Yet by the time I took the obligatory semi-annual physical, I had gotten used to the blank wall I met with when it came to my *real* families, my biological roots.

*   *   *

The first time this frustrating experience became really focused—only to be dismissed—occurred in 1944 when I was drafted into the U. S. Army. From then on, in many circumstances, the same questions arose: describe any serious, chronic diseases that your father or mother may have (or had); list the cause of your mother's and father's death. In due time I married and had four children. Eventually I realized that not only could I not respond factually to such questions, but also that at best I could provide for my children only half of their genetic heritage. More recently, with organ and bone transplants becoming a common fact of life, I further realized that if I were ever to need a donor who was a blood relative, I would be totally helpless.

Gradually, the conviction grew that I ought to make some effort to rectify this situation; I ought to discover, at the very least, my genetic background and something of the medical history of my biological family. This thought, however, never came to the fore until I found myself in Greeley, Colorado, in the summer of 1986. I had gone there to visit my widowed Aunt Mary Carson who was living in a nursing home. After the visit I had a few hours to myself. I was fairly sure that my adoption had taken place in Greeley; so it occurred to me, why not strike while the iron was hot. I suggested to my wife, therefore, that we go to the Weld County courthouse and see how much we could discover about my birth.

It wasn't long before I discovered one ineluctable fact—I wasn't going to find anything about my birth family as easily as I had supposed. The office of the Juvenile Court kept the adoption records. Beverly and I presented ourselves to the clerk on duty and made our request. The clerk was most pleasant and cooperative, up to a point. She politely informed me that she could not show me my adoption files unless she received a court order to that effect, signed by the appropriate judge. I had no time that day, however, to make an appointment with the proper judge; we were leaving Colorado within two days. I suggested that she take a peek inside the files to see if any sort of medical history existed. She brought the file to the counter and looked. "No," she said, "there's nothing here concerning the medical history of either you or your parents. I'm sorry," she added, and she returned the documents to the file folder.

Because my adoptive mother had told me years before what my given name at birth had been, I had fixed it in my mind. I had told Beverly that my name was Jack Walsh. As the folder lay on the counter, she was able to see the name identifying it. It was, indeed, Jack Walsh. One small but significant fact confirmed. We thanked the clerk for her help and left the courthouse.

This experience left my enthusiasm for the project more than a little dampened. I decided that I would probably not pursue my search any further. I discovered, however, that, unlike my attitude in the past, the desire to find my roots did not die. In the months following my frustrating experience in Greeley, I kept thinking, "Why should I give up so easily?" Surely the need to find my medical history, for my own benefit and that of my children, was of such importance that I could obtain a judge's order. During the following winter Beverly and I decided to return to Colorado the next summer to pursue the inquiry further. I would give myself several days to dig out the facts; meanwhile, I would find out which judge to contact and seek his assistance.

In the spring of 1987, however, I found myself frustrated again. After seeking legal counsel, I requested of my personal physician a brief statement to the effect that for a number of valid reasons the bearer of the letter be granted a judicial order allowing him to examine his adoption file. After many telephone calls to Colorado I finally was able to talk with a judge in the Weld County Juvenile Court. The conversation was long and detailed. The judge was knowledgeable and friendly. Ultimately, however, he proved to be discouraging, firmly maintaining that I would have little chance to get to my birth records. He pointed out that the confidentiality laws in the State of Colorado were extremely strict; the avenues to information of the kind I desired frustratingly narrow. For a number of years, he said, various legislators had offered bills to enable freer access to adoption records, but that the legislature had consistently defeated all such bills by significant margins. The protection of the privacy of the birth parents, that had initially motivated such legislation, was still of uppermost importance to current legislators. I asked him what type of special "case" it would require to receive a judicial order to open the file to me.

In reply he told about an actual case in which a particularly distraught couple had petitioned him to open the file of their daughter whom they had adopted when she was quite young. They had never informed her that she was an adopted child. She had no knowledge of this until the time came for her marriage, when, for some reason, it became expedient to inform her that she was not their own biological daughter. Her reaction had been extreme. At first she accused her adoptive parents of lying to her, not because they had not told her of her status but because she refused to believe that she was not their biological child. For some reason, best known to her, she believed that they had a sinister motive in telling her that she was not really theirs. Gradually it became evident that she needed professional psychiatric care. Upon the advice of the psychiatrist, the parents petitioned a judge to reveal the contents of the girl's adoption file. In this instance the judge granted the parents' request, which finally convinced the daughter, and the case ended happily. The point that the judge was making was clear. All I wanted was some simple medical records. Mine was not a case of life threatening psychosis; just simple curiosity. I thanked him for his counsel and the time he had taken with me and rang off.

What to do? Every avenue now seemed closed to me. After the frustration of the previous summer exacerbated by the brevity of my visit in Colorado, we planned a more extensive vacation in the West during the coming summer. Despite the judge's disheartening statements, we felt compelled to carry out our plan. Our daughter lived in Colorado Springs, an adoptive first cousin lived in Ft. Collins, and we had long-time family friends whom we wished to visit in Denver. An acquaintance of our daughter who lived in the mountains west of Colorado Springs needed house sitters for a week. We had secured a cabin on the Poudre River above Ft. Collins for another week. Our Denver friends invited us to stay with them for several days in the interim—a perfect time to organize a search for any kind of birth notice. Even though we had little expectation of finding much of value, we still anticipated the prospect of researching whatever records that might be available. We limited our search to four days, scarcely enough time to produce significant results. Meanwhile, a colleague at Geneva College whose avocation was genealogical research had given us some basic pointers to make our research easier.

*   *   *

We began our work in the Denver Public Library. At first it was slow going, for we were totally unfamiliar with the workings of the library, but we soon discovered the particular area in the library frequented by geneal-ogists (there were many of them) and, more encouragingly, the research librarians whose tireless efforts and remarkable patience in the face of our continuous questions made our work worthwhile. We began with the two Denver newspapers. *The Denver Post,* we soon discovered, did not record births during the 1920s. *The Rocky Mountain News* was more promising, for it recorded short lists of births almost daily. Finally, our patience was rewarded, for in the *News* of April 21, 1925, there appeared the following item: Joseph Walsh, 1460 Dexter St., boy. The date was one day after my birth. We had not expected this sort of lead. We were more excited than ever. Now, at last, we might find the promising trail we had so long hoped for.

When one begins genealogical research he discovers that there is a remarkable array of tools with which to carry on his task, some of them highly sophisticated, others very common. We soon discovered that we were entering what appeared to be a perfectly simple corridor of research, only to find that in reality we were in a maze. At times the single avenue created a dozen varied alleys and byways, and we had to explore each one. In every instance one had to pursue the lead carefully until it turned into a dead end or opened out upon a new avenue. In short, we found our-selves becoming detectives engaged in solving our own personal mystery story. What we discovered around every corner inevitably proved to be fas-cinating, although often frustrating as well. Following up the lead fur-nished by the *News,* we turned to the Denver city directory. This standard reference work lists every street in the city and records the name of every occupant—owner, renter, business, factory—at every given address on that street. This gave us the history of Joseph Walsh from 1924 until 1936 the time he lived at that address; sometime between 1936 and 1937 Joseph Walsh disappeared. The only record of his death would certainly be found in the office of Vital Statistics. (Later, in 1999, we discovered that to find his death certificate would cost $12.00. For obvious reasons that will appear below, we felt that to pay this amount was impractical.) His wife, Cora, remained at the address until sometime between 1942 and 1945. During that period the name of one child, William, appeared as well, but there was no listing for a Jack Walsh. We wondered why. Still, with the obvious birth announcement in the newspaper, we had to press on.

The Colorado Historical Society, located within walking distance of the library, became a source of great help. It was here that we discovered the "pleasures" of searching the census records. By law any given ten-year census record cannot become public domain for the next seventy years. Therefore, the most pertinent census records, those of 1920, were unavailable to us, and we were forced to rely on the 1910 census, hoping that the family might have lived at the same address a full fifteen years before my birth! As it turned out Cora and Joseph were not living at that address in 1910, for then Cora was unmarried and still living with her family.

We had discovered Cora's maiden name. The Hutcheson family lived nearby, and we were able to find the complete record of every member of this family. So, we were learning a great deal about the distaff side of the family—how many children, their sex and ages, the names of the father and mother and where they had come from. We began to get a "feel" for the family. I found myself thinking of myself as a Walsh, and to a degree a Hutcheson, for the first time in my life. An identity was slowly forming in my mind. Still, there was no concrete evidence of a Jack Walsh no matter where we looked; I was still in reality a nonentity.

Two more viable avenues of research opened up to us. Because of Joseph Walsh's "disappearance" we assumed his death to have occurred in or around 1936. We walked to the Denver County Court House to see if we could determine his death with certainty. Upon filling out the proper forms we eventually received a small file positively identified with this particular man, only to find that in 1936 he had not died but had been committed by Cora to the Colorado Psychopathic Hospital, a hospital commonly used to process mental patients. There was no further record. Here, we realized, was a new, vaguely ominous, fact. One motive for my search had been to discover my genetic background; now, perhaps, I was finding something more than I had expected, something that I might not be able to handle. Well-meaning friends had warned us from the outset that just this sort of "surprise" might occur. "I wouldn't pursue that search, if I were you, Norm," some of my friends had teasingly warned, "you might turn up a horse thief in the family!" There would be the knowing laugh. It was a standard joke, of course, but behind the levity was an unmistakable air of seriousness as well. What to do now?

We decided that the least we could do was to visit the hospital, now a part of the University of Colorado Health Services Center, to see if they had any record of Joseph Walsh's commitment. In considering the absolute wall of secrecy we had met when it came to my adoption files, we scarcely expected the results we obtained when we visited the hospital.

I introduced myself to a friendly employee.

"Are there records still available of persons committed to the hospital in the years past?" I asked.

"Yes," she answered, "there are; not very complete, but perhaps worth something by way of information. Although the person in charge of the records is away today, I can probably make a preliminary search for you."

Then, with little ado, the friendly woman dug into the proper drawer filled with 3 x 5 cards, extracting the necessary card. The card contained very little information, but what was there at least provided some measure of relief: Joseph had been committed with a serious case of alcoholism and, within days, had been released.

Did I prefer alcoholism to "mental illness" in my genetic background? It didn't take long to answer that question. Apart from a brief period in my youth, I had never drunk anything alcoholic, and at this point, because of the ordination vows laid on me as an ordained officer of my denomination, I was a teetotaler. The genetic possibilities, therefore, were relatively insignificant, but the answer to Joseph Walsh's disappearance from the face of the earth was no closer.

We decided to try another avenue of research. We could trace the William Walsh who appeared in the record. We turned to the simplest tool of research, the telephone book. The library had copies of every Denver Metropolitan telephone directory back to the early 1930s. Eventually we found the name of Mrs. Cora Walsh in the directory, living at the proper address. Through many years William Walsh's name also appeared there. Eventually his name disappeared; then hers. We deduced, incorrectly as it turned out, that Cora had died. William Walsh's name appeared, however, in the telephone directory at a Washington Ave. address. As we scanned the successive directories, eventually the entry read Mrs. William Walsh. Perhaps he had died as well.

School records often furnish valuable information, but we hadn't pursued that particular byway, so the next day we decided to try it. Although we had ascertained that Cora had attended a public high school in Denver, the Walsh family proved to be Roman Catholic.

Our next step was to visit the diocesan Office of Catholic Schools on Josephine St. to make inquiry about any William Walsh who might have enrolled in some Catholic school. The secretary, who proved to be extremely busy, told us that our search might prove to be fruitless. Somehow we were able to convince her that we had very little time left to spend in Denver and that we would not trouble her again if an initial search turned up nothing. She returned shortly with one piece of valuable information. "Yes," she pointed out, "here is a William Walsh, son of Joseph and Cora Walsh who attended Regis High School and matriculated at Regis College." We thanked the secretary and, armed with this information, continued to the diocesan office itself. If William Walsh had attended Regis College, alumni records might prove conclusively whether he was, indeed, the same William Walsh whose name we had been finding in the telephone directory. However, although we were given positive

information that he had attended Regis College, no further information was available.

We had been conducting our pursuit for two and a half days. It was time to take a lunch break, and as my wife and I sat together over our tuna fish salads and ice tea, we decided that it was time to take radical action. We had no proof that the Mrs. William Walsh was, indeed, the widow of the William Walsh we had been researching. We might be going up a dead end street. We could return to another avenue, or we could take the chance that our guess was correct and call the woman.

An extremely nervous caller stood at the restaurant pay phone. I had rehearsed very briefly in my mind just what approach I would take, but when the pleasant voice on the other end of the line answered I panicked.

"Hello," I said; then, wondering where my confidence had suddenly gone, pressed on. I gave my name, trying to sound as authentic and unthreatening as possible. "I'm here in Denver for a few days, doing genealogical research, and I wondered if I might ask you a few questions?"

"Why, yes," she replied, "what is it that I can help you with?" Her voice remained reasonably friendly. I took heart.

"Well, first, I probably should tell you that I am an adopted child. My original name was Walsh." I kept pouring out the facts. No use to let her insert a quick disclaimer before I could lay a significant amount of information on the table. She seemed genuinely interested.

"And you think that there is some possible connection between yourself and my husband?" she asked.

"Possibly," I replied. "Please excuse my boldness, but am I right to assume that he is deceased?"

"Yes, he died a number of years ago." She gave no evidence of being troubled by my personal question.

"The William Walsh that I'm interested in," I continued hastily, "was the son of Joseph and Cora Hutcheson Walsh who lived on Dexter Street." I paused.

"Well, you've certainly hit the right spot," she said, "those are my husband's parents."

By now I was becoming excited. It was time for the telling question. Still, because I couldn't bring myself to ask it straight out, I chose the oblique approach. "The most mysterious aspect of my search, Mrs. Walsh," I said, "is that there seem to have been other children in the family, but I haven't been able to trace anyone but your husband. Could you tell me if he had brothers or sisters?"

Her reply was also indirect. "I find this really exciting. To think that William might have had another brother that he never told me about." She continued, "But I can tell you of one other brother that I knew. Raymond's gone now, but he was about twelve years younger than William."

"Oh. Raymond, you say?" I was doing rapid mental calculation as I talked.

"Yes, Raymond. I never knew him very well. He was nice person. As I said, he was about twelve years my husband's junior."

By that time I had completed my mental arithmetic, and I didn't like what it added up to. My heart dropped to my shoes. Raymond, by simple calculation, had been born in 1925, and because there was no record of twins, the inference was obvious. I was not Raymond. I was someone else! The family I had been researching was not mine! For nearly three days of intensive research I had been barking up the wrong family tree. I expressed my deep personal chagrin to Mrs. Walsh as calmly as I could.

"Never mind," she replied. "I'm sorry that it seems to point that way, but why don't you pursue it just a bit further? I'm sure that you can find Raymond's baptismal record among the parish records. Look that up, why don't you, just to be absolutely sure. And call me tomorrow," she added, "I really am interested in your research, and I'd like to know what you find out."

At that point we had little taste for further research, but we decided to visit the parish house and see if the records bore out our deduction. The sister who greeted us was most kind and soon produced the proper baptismal record ledger. Sure enough, there he was—Raymond Walsh—born April 10, 1925, ten days before my birth. Our assumption that the newspaper would record the birth a day later proved to be very wrong. About two hours remained that afternoon until all public offices closed. We tried to think of a way to use that precious time to the best advantage and decided to go to the Bureau of Vital Statistics and make application to recover my original birth certificate.

*   *   *

At every turn during the three days' search officials told us that such a task was a virtual impossibility. Every person with whom we came in contact parroted the opinion rendered informally by the judge earlier in the year—the pleasant but firmly negative bureaucrat in the Weld County Juvenile Court, the concerned young woman at the Home Services, Inc. Administration where the Florence Crittenden Home kept their official records, and the sympathetic research librarians at the library. They even supplied their own horror story of an individual, wheeled up one day to their counter, able to breathe only through the aid of an oxygen tank, who was desperately seeking information that would lead to her birth family. Even she, in a condition *in extremis* had been denied the necessary court order.

We entered the records office of the Bureau praying that we might receive some miraculous break. I filled out the form necessary to obtain my birth certificate. I gave my original name and date of birth Next I gave my own name, my relationship to the person whose certificate I sought, and the reason for my request. I decided that my approach would have to be straightforward. I simply wrote that I was "Jack Walsh" and briefly explained why I sought the certificate. The young woman at the window took the form, glanced at it, smiled with what I assumed was sympathy and announced, "We aren't allowed to do this, you know."

I sighed and said that, assuredly, I did know, but that I had decided to try anyhow. "Even if I were allowed to do this," she continued, "the chances are extremely slim that I could find the certificate. You see," she said, "several years ago, all the original birth certificates of adopted persons were pulled and placed in a sealed vault for protection."

I thought to myself, yes, protection from dishonest con artists, crooks, and self-serving opportunists—troublemakers. I also realized that caught in that maze of legal red tape and bureaucratic stonewalling were persons like myself who had no sinister ulterior motives but only the sincere desire to obtain vital information about themselves.

"You could go round the corner to the office of Adoptees In Search," the clerk added. She really was trying to help, although her hands were tied. "They can perhaps get you started on the process of finding your family. It *has* been done." She glanced over my shoulder to the person standing patiently in line behind me; the interview was over. With an overwhelming sense of frustration, I moved away.

The visit to the Adoptees In Search office proved to be of little help. Yes, they did help adoptees find their birth families. Yes, it was sometimes successful. The catch was that the family, or a member of the family, had also to have placed a request with them as well. We knew that the chances of that having happened were virtually non existent. We took the pamphlet offered to us and left the building.

That evening we were as depressed as two researchers could be. Things certainly could be worse. I thought of scholars that I had known who had lost significant portions of their research through a computer glitch or all of their research through a fire or even a bankrupt printing company. My attempt to cheer Beverly was only partly successful. I took her out to dinner at a cozy Greek restaurant after calling Mrs. Walsh one final time. "Come to visit me anyway," she said. On the basis of our extremely brief and invisible acquaintance, she was a genuinely pleasant person. I have often thought of her since, wondering if she might not be interested in what followed the next day.

We returned to our hosts, the McBurneys, who had expressed great interest in our project but who, on hearing the latest discouraging news, provided the encouragement we sorely needed. The following day we determined at least to start from scratch with an optimistic spirit, although we felt that realistically there was little hope. Again we returned to the Denver Public Library. Again we searched the *Rocky Mountain News*. Perhaps we had overlooked an entry. Again we were unsuccessful. As time passed and we stopped for lunch we realized that we had exactly twenty-four hours remaining to find something, exactly the same amount of time we had taken the year before when we made our initial inquiry in Greeley. We discussed the situation over lunch. "I'm desperate at this point," and I looked desperately at my wife.

"You know what they say," she replied, "desperate circumstances require desperate means."

"Yeah," I said, "but how desperate do we want to get?"

"I've been thinking." She hesitated a moment before offering her desperate solution. "You know, I think we really ought to try the Bureau one more time."

"But we didn't get anywhere, remember?"

"What if?" She grinned. "What if we filled out the form again, but this time you pretended to be someone *related* to Jack Walsh, which you *are*." She paused, trying out the plan on me. "But you wouldn't say that it was an exact identity." She looked at me and waited. She knew what my first reaction would be. We all practice deceit at various times in our lives, despite our best efforts. We simply try to avoid deliberate, conscious deceit when we are tempted. I was well aware that my life was not a faultless record when it came to telling the truth, but my tendency had always been—and Beverly knew it—to be as scrupulously honest as I could be.

"That would be lying, Bev. You know that."

"I *knew* you'd say that," she admitted," but I think that we're *never* going to get anywhere at all unless we try it. You're never going to get that court order based on your request, as honest as you are. The straightforward, legitimate route seems hopeless on the surface. I just think we ought to give it one more try. If the certificate is locked in a vault, in the long run we probably won't succeed anyway."

"Well, you're right about that," I said. "I've a queer feeling about attempting it, but let's try it."

Although I definitely felt guilty, my last scruple had dropped away. I just couldn't face the prospect of never knowing who I really was. We entered the Bureau of Vital Statistics again, this time feeling more like novice bank robbers. I took the form and started to fill it out. I was going to state that I was Jack Walsh's stepbrother. As I filled out the form, however, I grew increasingly nervous. Suppose the same woman whom I confronted the day before turned up at the window? Her memory might be short; then, again, it might not. I decided that I couldn't take that chance. I turned to Beverly and asked her if she would like to try out her acting skills.

"Meaning what?"

"Look! Suppose that same gal is at the window. She just might recognize me. If she does, we've really blown it for good."

"What do you have in mind, then?"

"Why don't *you* fill out the form instead of me. I'll just wait around the corner." Nothing like being chicken at the last moment, I thought, but it might be less risky. We had no idea about which relationship would bear fruit and at the same time remain essentially true. Later, a friend suggested that Beverly could have claimed to have been Jack's first wife, a remarkable bit of sophistry, but we weren't thinking along sophisticated lines of argument at that point.

"O.K." I said, "Just identify yourself as his step-sister." It was the best ploy I could come up with in a pinch.

Beverly gave the idea some thought and sighed, "Well, all right. Give me the form."

We discarded the half-filled out form, got another and completed it. There were a number of persons at each of the three windows, and Beverly took the form to the window where, she judged, she might have the greatest chance of succeeding, a window manned this time by a bright young man who looked as if he might be a college student on temporary summertime employment. The dreaded clerk was seated inside the office busily working at her desk. Meanwhile, like the coward I was, I retreated to a spot sufficiently distant to see Beverly without being seen by anyone in the office. I felt increasingly like a cloak-and-dagger conspirator. I was, by then, as nervous as a doctoral candidate, awaiting the decision of his oral defense committee.

Of course, my nervousness was nothing compared to Beverly's. Acting had never been her forte, and never had she possessed nerves of steel. She kept her head down, hand partially shielding her face from the view of the clerk at the desk, and pushed the form across the counter toward the young man. Moreover, she was quite worried by this time, for she had heard the clerk tell the applicant immediately before her that his being the husband of the party who wished a certificate was not enough; the applicant had to be a blood relative. So much for the "first wife" ploy. The clerk took her form and disappeared. The wait seemed interminable. The clerk had *not* rejected her application, but would the certificate have vanished, locked securely, forever in the vault? To Beverly's surprise, the clerk reappeared, carrying in his hand the copy of a birth certificate. Beverly paid the requisite ten dollar fee, and the certificate was ours. She whipped around the corner, waving the piece of paper and whispering in her best conspiratorial tone, "Let's get out of here—now!"

*   *   *

As we sat in the car, blazing hot from the afternoon sun, I held the certificate in my hand, scarcely realizing the import of that moment. There it was, at last! There was the information I had so long desired: My name, correct; my date of birth, correct; my father's name, my mother's maiden name, their ages; where each had come from; their Denver residence;

where the birth had taken place; and the name and office address of the attending physician. There was, however, one glaring error—I was identified as "female!" Beverly and I looked at each other and began to laugh, partly because of the obvious error, but mostly out of a huge sense of relief. We had done it! We believed firmly that in reality we hadn't compromised our ethical convictions. Still, at that moment we asked God's forgiveness and drove away.

We realized that there was much yet to do. Enough time remained for our return to the Denver Public Library and at least to begin to fill in the missing pieces.

One interesting piece was the existence of the Denver Maternity Hospital where I had been born. The Business Directory told us that this particular institution had ceased to exist in 1939. We decided to drive to the address in the near northwest section of the city to see if there were any remains of the building. Before we left we checked out the City Directory to discover what residents had lived where my parents had lived, but there were precious few clues to follow. It appeared that many people had lived in that particular building. It stood at 827 22nd St. at the corner of Champa and 22nd St., and appeared to be a transient residence. So it proved to be.

We drove to the spot and discovered that, for many years, the building, constructed in 1904, had been a transient hotel originally named the Marrato. It still stood, surrounded by acres of wasteland, largely used as parking lots. A FOR SALE sign covered the name embossed in concrete above the top floor. The building, however, retained some of its original character. At one time, long ago, it may have been one of the more attractive sites in the area. Now, it stood as a lone survivor of urban blight. (In 1999, upon visiting this spot again, I discovered that there was more activity in the neighborhood than before, perhaps because of its near proximity to Coors Field. The building stood there, much the same. It had, sometime in the interim, housed Muddy's Java Cafe and Bookstore, but that too had failed to survive the years, and the building was again up for sale.)

From there we turned westward on 23rd St., past a skid row section of Denver, and over a bridge that crossed a great stretch of rail yard to that section of the city where the maternity hospital had been. When we arrived at 2417 W. 32nd Ave., imagine our surprise to find it still there but not the building we had imagined. Instead of a brick, three-story building occupying half a city block, there stood a moderately large, two-story frame house, very recently refurbished. It could easily have been a modest maternity facility, for the recently installed mailboxes visible on the front porch indicated that now there were seven separate dwelling units. In contrast to the transient hotel, the onetime maternity home had easily survived the transition and made an attractive contribution to its neighborhood.

In our last hours in the library we found ourselves trying to trace the whereabouts of the physician who had delivered me. Dr. George Achison proved to have been a well-known physician with a solid reputation. The office address on the certificate was almost illegible. We engaged in some fairly wild searching and finally found a simple answer; his office had once occupied number 405 in the Tabor Opera House Building at 16th and Champa Streets in downtown Denver.

The most significant piece of information, however, that we found that last day in the library we discovered again in that most common genealogical source—the telephone book. The library collection of Denver telephone directories over the years was not only surprisingly complete, but in addition there were directories from cities in every corner of the land. My birth certificate stated that both my father and mother had come from Las Vegas, New Mexico, and there in the collection was a current Las Vegas directory. My mother's maiden name was Elizabeth Hurt. We searched for any Walshes or Hurts in the book. We found no Walshes, but there was one Hurt listed. We took down the number, closing out our four days of research and left Denver.

*   *   *

We felt that our next step was obvious, but I was not at that point up to calling another complete stranger, especially after the disappointing results of the previous call. I had to think about this for a time. This required some strategy. We drove to our daughter's home in Colorado Springs and put the question of the call out of our minds for a time. We laid the whole matter before God. That evening we prayed that He would lead in a very specific way as I talked with the Mr. Hurt listed in the directory; that He would give me the precise words I needed. We asked God to provide through this stranger access to the information I had so long pursued.

The following day I called Las Vegas. Even though I had just experienced a similar conversation in Denver, I was as nervous as before, perhaps more so, for I felt that here, at last, might be the key I desired. A man's voice—soft-spoken and gentle—answered my call. I asked if I was speaking to Mr. William Hurt. He replied that, indeed, I was. I had decided the night before that I couldn't handle a direct approach and that perhaps he couldn't either. So, I thought, an oblique approach would be the best way to begin. I introduced myself.

"Mr. Hurt," I said, "I'm calling from Colorado Springs. I've been in Colorado doing some genealogical research for the past week, and my search has led me to call you for further information. Do you mind my asking you some questions?"

He assured me that he did not.

"Would you, by any chance, know of an Elizabeth Hurt who once lived in Las Vegas, New Mexico?" I asked.

The answer came immediately. "Yes, I do. She's my sister."

My hand shook. How to continue? It took me several minutes before it began to sink in that I was actually talking to my own uncle. However, I kept bravely on. I had committed myself. I had to continue.

"Mr. Hurt, this next question is a very difficult one to ask, but are you, or have you ever been, aware that your sister may have given up a child for adoption years ago? Is that possible?" I waited for his answer.

This time he was more hesitant, yet his answer seemed revealing. "Well," he replied slowly, "she *may* have." No unequivocal "yes," but no unequivocal "no" either.

It was now time to bring the facts on the birth certificate into the conversation. "Did she live in Denver in the 1920s?"

"Yes."

"Was she married then to a man named Harry Walsh?"

His answer came as a shock. "Yes, she was married to Harry, but his name wasn't Walsh; it was Wells."

Oh, no, I thought, not again. Still, I pursued the matter. "Were your sister and Harry living in Denver, specifically in the years 1924-1926?"

"Yes."

"And Harry Walsh—Wells—would he have been about ten years older than your sister? Was he an accountant?" The answer to both questions was affirmative. There was now no doubt in my mind. This man, Harry Wells, was in all likelihood my father. Elizabeth Hurt was, indeed, my mother. Of that there could be no question. Now it was time to ask the crucial question. Even oblique approaches *are*, after all, only approaches, and I found that I could no longer avoid telling this man what I now knew as a certainty.

"Mr. Hurt." I paused, hardly daring to continue. My voice shook and seemed at the point of failing me altogether. "Mr. Hurt, I have reason to believe that your sister did give up a child for adoption in 1925, and that I am that child."

I cannot now remember his response, but I soon realized that he was not going to hang up on me or even consider my statement outrageous and dismiss my claim. The conversation continued, even becoming more natural as he revealed the salient facts about my family.

He told me that I had a sister in Argentina and a brother in Oklahoma. For some reason, however, possibly because my news was sufficiently overwhelming for him, he failed to mention that I had another brother in New Mexico. He told me that Harry and Betty Wells had lived in Denver for three years; then returned to New Mexico, first to Las Vegas, then to the tiny village of San Juan Pueblo, north of Santa Fe. He described my father's occupation as an accountant for the firm of Ruth and Kramer Mercantile Inc., a general store in the pueblo. I learned that my father had died in 1962, that my mother had remarried and moved to the state of Washington, that her second husband had died recently, and that she was still living! This was more than I had ever hoped for.

"Where is she now?" I asked.

"Well," my uncle said, "she's living with her sister in Roswell."

I pursued my inquiry. "Do you think she would mind if I wrote to her?" I asked.

"No," he assured me, "go ahead. I don't think she would mind at all."

Still, I was hesitant about this step, enough to ask him twice more during our conversation if he thought it would be a mistake to write to her. Each time he reassured me. I decided that I must write. There really wasn't much more to say at this point. His interest was obviously genuine. I was sure that I recognized a kind of acceptance of me shown in that conversation. This proved to be true as I came to know him much more extensively through the following months. We agreed to keep in touch.

I turned to Beverly who had been listening to my end of the conversation. "You won't believe it, Bev," I said, "but my mother is still alive. The man I just talked to is my Uncle Bill. I've inherited a whole new family!"

At her suggestion, we, along with our daughter who was trying to assimilate the news herself, celebrated the news in a modest way that night. Both Rebecca and Beverly insisted that I write to my mother, explaining who I was and suggesting that we get in touch. I agreed, but I knew that this would be one of the most difficult letters I would ever write, for I had to write with the utmost tact. Because Uncle Bill had hinted that she was not well, I had to avoid shocking her. I had to reassure her that I had no ulterior motives. Above all, I had to establish a tone in the letter: friendly, but not too friendly; inquisitive, but not too personal; serious, but not overbearing.

I devoted the entire next day to writing that letter. My daughter did own a rather long-of-tooth typewriter; so I decided that I would write the letter in longhand, revise it as much as necessary, and then type it. The first draft flowed rather easily; the revisions were much more difficult. I had to examine each statement carefully to see if I were making unwarranted requests or if any statement even hinted at offense. Rebecca owned nothing so sophisticated as a computer, and her typewriter had to be one of the most recalcitrant and awkward machines I had ever worked with. Still, I finished the letter by mid-afternoon, and, with a prayer, sent it off to Roswell. I was certain that the contents would be startling enough to give my mother pause, so I struggled to make it as genuinely harmless as possible. How to address my mother? Mrs. Lague? Mother? I finally decided on Elizabeth:

Dear Elizabeth,

This will be an extremely difficult letter for me to write. I have no idea how you will react to what I have to say nor how you will respond to my request for information, but I trust that your response will be positive.

May I assure you immediately that in no sense do I want to elicit information from you which you do not wish to divulge, despite the nature of some of my inquiry. Nor do I want to cause you any pain nor grief brought on by what could be disturbing memories. Again, I sincerely trust that the passage of time will have worked in you a peace about events in the distant past and that you might actually want to share something of your life with me. In that regard, I intend voluntarily to provide (below) some information about myself that may be of interest to you. Furthermore, I have absolutely **no** ulterior motive related to money, property or the like. You may count on my integrity in that regard.

Let me begin then by stating that I have known since childhood that I was an adopted child. For many years I had not one iota of curiosity about my blood parents. Forty-five years ago I was told by my adoptive mother what my original name was—Jack Walsh. I was born in Denver, April 20, 1925. About fifteen years ago I began to realize that the lack of knowledge about my blood parents was (and would continue to be) presenting a real problem. Each time I faced certain physical examinations I was unable to answer any questions relating to my inherited genetic characteristics. And, of course, to a significant degree, the same is true for my children and grandchildren.

So, three years ago I made inquiry in Weld Co., Colorado, where my adoption took place, but found I was unable to obtain the information I needed. I did confirm my birth name, however. I was in Colorado for too brief a time to pursue it further.

This July I returned for a four-week vacation. My wife and I have spent about four days in Denver researching this problem. The break came just last Tuesday when we were able, by some nearly miraculous circumstance, to obtain my birth certificate.

The certificate revealed the following: Jack Walsh, born to Harry Walsh (27) and Elizabeth Hurt (17), April 20, 1925. Birth at the Denver Maternity Hospital, 2417 W. 32nd Ave. Attending physician, Dr. George Atchison, Tabor Building, Denver. Harry Walsh's given residence, 827 22nd St., Denver (a rooming house or boarding house?) and his occupation, accountant. Both parents were born in Las Vegas, New Mexico.

We could find no trace in the Householder Directory of a Harry Walsh living at the above address, a mystery which was later cleared up by a telephone call I made to a W. C. Hurt of Las Vegas.

It took me a full day to get enough courage (brass?) to call Mr. Hurt. His was the only Hurt name in the Las Vegas telephone directory. I finally did so because I was to leave Colorado on Friday, August 21, for my home in Pennsylvania.

I do not know whether your brother has called you or not. Perhaps he has. I do not know for sure how much he knew of your early life. I understand that he is three years younger than you. But I pray that you will not be angry nor disappointed with him nor with me because of his giving me much valuable information. He was most gracious in providing it, citing the fact that his own daughter had adopted children, and so he understood my dilemma. About your early life and early years of marriage he was properly vague. He did tell me that your first husband was Harry Wells, not Walsh, but every other fact contained in the certificate he confirmed—except, of course, my actual birth.

This left me with no recourse then but to write this letter to you. I have worried about its impact on you, for I don't know the state of your health or emotional condition. I asked your brother three times if he thought you would mind. He always insisted that you would not.

Let me give you now some pertinent information about myself. I am, of course, now 62 years old. I was adopted by a Greeley clergyman and his wife, Rev. Charles T. Carson and May F. Carson. As a result of the effects of the Spanish Influenza (1917) my adoptive mother could not have children. I assume the adoption was arranged between my parents' physician and, perhaps, Dr. Atchison.

I grew up in Sterling, Kansas, and attended college in Pennsylvania. Subsequently, I received an M. A. and a Ph. D. degree in English, and for nearly 30 years I have been teaching English in a small, denominational college (Geneva) in Pennsylvania. I also graduated from a Presbyterian seminary, am an ordained minister and at one time pastored a congregation in Chicago.

I have been married for 34 years and have four children and three grandchildren. I would be happy to tell you more, if you so desire.

What I am most interested in receiving from you, Elizabeth, is 1) medical histories from your family and that of Harry Wells; then 2) permission to continue our correspondence if it pleases you; finally 3) if you really want it, a chance to meet you and other family members personally in the near future—again **only** if you are interested. It is a scary proposition, I know, and I do not intend pursuing the 2nd and 3rd steps unless and until you request these. It would, however, be extremely frustrating to me if I cannot obtain medical information.

What I am interested in (subject of course to the the limits of **your** willingness to divulge details) are such things as:

1) the cause of Harry Wells' death

2) occurrences of such conditions in the families as diabetes, cancer, heart disease, any other chronic debilitating condition, **including** anything you might know of hereditary conditions.

It would be of great importance to me to find out such things. Bear in mind, too, that I need to know contributing factors (for example, did Harry Wells use tobacco or drink heavily or was he overweight?)

Now, if you agree with me that we ought to pursue our correspondence further; then, for example, I would like to send you copies of photos of me as a boy or in later years, or tell you of some of my natural talents (such as they are) which might have been inherited from either of you.

This has been a long letter, but I trust it has not disturbed you to read it. My whole life has been wrapped up totally in my adoptive family. In a real sense I can scarcely think of myself or my family as anything other than Carson. I hope you will understand that. Yet, now that I apparently know finally who my blood relatives are, I am filled with a mixture of relief and apprehension.

I am most anxious to hear from you. I hope you will write soon.

Sincerely,

I really didn't expect to receive a reply in less than a month. A few days later we returned to Pennsylvania and to the new collegiate year. A month passed. Then two, and three. My mother's reply never came. What had her reaction been? Traumatic shock? Anger? Wouldn't one expect a *mother* especially to react positively, now that she knew for certain that her baby had survived and had had a good life? Was she too ill to write? We asked all these questions through the fall and the winter months. Still no letter. Occasionally I would call my uncle in New Mexico. Yes, Betty wasn't very well. He had intended to drive to Roswell to see her; then he would find out what her reaction had been, but he wasn't in the best of health himself, so he just hadn't done it. He promised me that he would visit the sisters, approach my Aunt Carroll first to see what the lay of the land was; then talk to Betty. I had to be satisfied with that. The wait was long. Not until that summer was I to get the break I had been waiting for.

3

I Learn to Spell Albuquerque

Having fully expected my mother to answer my letter within a few weeks at most, my expectations gradually waned, and by Christmas of 1987 I had finally come to the realization that I was probably not going to hear from her at all. I had turned to my well-worn highway atlas and looked up San Juan Pueblo and Las Vegas, to see where my parents had lived. I realized that I knew two Geneva College alumni living in New Mexico. One of them, Margaret Franke, an English major from the 1960s, lived in Truches, high in the New Mexico mountains. She and her husband, Bill, had moved there several years earlier, and she was now teaching English at Northern New Mexico Community College in nearby Espanola. Both towns were within shouting distance of San Juan. Perhaps, someone related to the Wells family still lived in the neighborhood. I decided to call her to see if she could provide useful information.

My relationship with Margaret and Bill had remained strong over the years. She had come to Geneva College from a farm a few miles from our home, and I still dropped by occasionally to fish in the quarry on their property and to chat with her parents. Without hesitation, therefore, I called her.

"Hi, Margaret!" I announced, "Surprised to hear from me?" I thought, why shouldn't she be? I hadn't called her in years.

"Well," she answered, "long time no hear. What brings this on?"

"Margaret, I need some help. I'm doing some interesting genealogical research." My approach was beginning to sound like a broken record. Didn't I have a more innovative opening than this?

"Sounds interesting. What can I do for you?"

"I don't know, exactly," I replied. I then told her what had happened over the past three months. "It appears that I have New Mexico connections," I continued, "and because my parents once lived near your town, I wonder if you could discover anything about them. Do you know many people in the community?"

She assured me that she did and that she would pursue the matter. "In fact," she added, almost as an afterthought, "I do know someone named Parker Wells, a semi-retired teacher in the vicinity, who does some teaching at the Community College. I'll get back to you whenever I find anything of interest."

This information certainly seemed promising. Here, perhaps, was a cousin. Uncle Bill had never mentioned him. I didn't have long to wait. Within two weeks Margaret returned my call.

"Norman," she began, "this Parker Wells seems to be connected with the family as far as I can determine." She increased my interest by telling me that she and Bill had attended a football game the previous Friday night and that Parker Wells's son, Ken, was a member of the team. Parker had been there. "You know, Norman," she added with a chuckle, "Bill and I got a good look at him, and we agree that he looks very much like you!"

"Margaret," I asked, "how good are you at playing detective?"

"Never done it," she answered, "but if you want me to…"

"See what you can find out. I'll get back to you."

Beverly and I had a great deal to mull over by this time. Who could this Parker Wells be? Uncle Bill had mentioned a brother of his who lived in Denver and the aunt with whom my mother was living, but he had told me nothing about the Wells side of the family. I decided that it was time to call him again.

This time my uncle filled in a number of details that had been tantalizingly absent before, including the fact that, indeed, I had *two* brothers, Sam, already mentioned, and Parker. Apparently I had startled him enough by my initial telephone call that he omitted Parker's name. This particular piece of news only sharpened my desire to discover more about the Wells family through my Truches detective. Thus began a series of calls that extended through the spring of 1988. In each conversation Margaret would relay tiny bits of new information. She apologized for not moving faster but explained that she didn't want to spook the prey.

She confirmed my father's death but hadn't been able to discover the cause. A fire had destroyed the general store a number of years earlier. Nothing of it remained in the pueblo. Eventually she sent a copy of a publicity brochure published by the college where Parker's photograph appeared, taken as he counseled a student. The tiny, somewhat indistinct picture was clear enough to confirm Margaret's opinion; Parker Wells *did* look like me. For the first time in my life I was looking at the likeness of my biological brother. Although the impact was strange and exciting, it sank in very slowly. Margaret next sent a copy of a page from the college yearbook where a more formal photograph of Parker appeared. More confirmation! Furthermore, she had discovered that there was a Wells, a woman in her nineties, living in a nearby nursing home. Perhaps a relative; she wasn't sure. One of her acquaintances had referred to a cousin's wife, Dr. Frances Hernandez, an English professor at the University of Texas in El Paso. Moreover, this cousin was someone Margaret had met occasionally at professional meetings.

Finally, Margaret informed me that she had had an opportunity to talk directly with Parker. He had requested a favor of her, and when he came to her office, she had taken the opportunity—delicately she said— to question him a bit about his family, particularly about his father. Later, I discovered that this line of questioning had recurred several times and had so mystified Parker that he spoke of it to his wife who, laughing softly, teasingly inquired if this Margaret "had a thing" for him.

*   *   *

A turning point occurred in June of 1988. The holiday season was six months past, and Uncle Bill had still not satisfied my curiosity about my mother's "reluctance" to reply to my letter. Even though I was gradually becoming vicariously acquainted with Parker, I had determined that I would not write to any of my siblings so long as my mother failed to respond to my letter. It could very well be that throughout the years she had never told any of them of my existence, and that she did not want them to know that she had given up a child. I felt that it would be a breach of ethics to write to any of them under these circumstances. As long as this situation existed, I was stymied in my search.

Again I called Uncle Bill. I had just enough hope to try again. Perhaps he had gone to Roswell very recently. Maybe he knew something this time. His reply was gentle, but the news he conveyed came as a shock. My mother had died only two days before. He was intending to call or write within a day or so. She had, it appeared, been more ill than either he had known or had chosen to reveal. My immediate reaction was twofold: great disappointment that I would never see my biological mother and relief that I would now be able to write to someone else in the family. There was no longer any need to hide the facts. Uncle Bill was unable to tell me much more at this point. He described, however, my mother's life with her second husband, Gomer Lague, a former milling company salesman and agricultural consultant. Apparently, my mother had enjoyed a happy twenty-four years of marriage, living in the state of Washington and travelling widely over the globe.

Uncle Bill insisted that I should come for a visit if I ever got out West again, and I promised that I would. For now the most important matter at hand was the composition of another letter introducing myself to my family. I wondered if this letter would be any more successful than the first had been. To whom would I write? It would have to be one of the siblings, and so I chose Parker, the brother whom I "knew" yet didn't know.

I wrote this letter in much the same tone as I had my first. The last thing I wanted was to scare the family off. I gingerly tried to reassure Parker that I had absolutely no ulterior motive in introducing myself and making my inquiries. I explained that I had reached the family through Uncle Bill; at the same time I scrupulously avoided referring to Margaret Franke. It wouldn't do to spoil their otherwise pleasant professional relationship. Maybe later, but not now. At least I had an excellent typewriter this time. I wrote:

Dear Parker:

This will have to be a carefully written letter for reasons that will become clear to you shortly. Also it will be one of the most difficult letters I have ever written, certainly as difficult as a letter I wrote to your mother last August.

Permit me to introduce myself. My name is Norman Carson. I am a professor of English at Geneva College, Beaver Falls, Pennsylvania. I have resided in Pennsylvania, more or less continuously for the past 47 years. Prior to 1941 I lived in central Kansas, but I was born in Denver, Colorado. Now for the shocker.

I am an adopted child, adopted by my parents in July, 1925, in Greeley, Colorado. Until the last few years I accepted this fact and loved my parents dearly, so much in fact that never did I wish to discover my blood heritage. I still love them in that way and think of them of course as my family. But more and more often I have been confronted by the bald fact that I can never ascertain with certainty my genetic nor my medical history. So, last summer I set out to see if I could discover enough about my blood parents so that I, my children and my grandchildren could have this heretofore absent knowledge. Through a series of remarkable circumstances I was able to obtain my original birth certificate. I therefore have what seems incontrovertable evidence that your mother and my blood mother are the same person. This, in fact, would make us brothers or at least half brothers, but I am strongly inclined to think it is the former.

At this point you may wish to catch your breath. I would not blame you. But let me proceed. My adoptive mother told me years ago that my original name was JACK WALSH. I was born in Denver on April 20, 1925, which makes me 63 now. Last summer, although I was unable to look into my adoptive file in Colorado, I was able to confirm my birth name on the outside of the file. As I mentioned, I then secured my birth certificate. The information there included the following: Father, Harry Walsh, age 27; home, Las Vegas, N.M.; Mother, Elizabeth Hurt, age 17; home Las Vegas, N.M; father's occupation, accountant; place of child's birth (the address proved to be the Denver Maternity Hospital, now long defunct); residence of the parents, the address which appears to have been a transient lodging place at the corner of 22nd and Champa Sts. in Denver. The physician's name was signed as well. He died a number of years ago but was apparently a well-known physician who had his offices in the Tabor Opera building in downtown Denver. The strangest "fact" on the certificate was this: I was listed as "female"!

The other strange "fact" was, of course, my father's last name, something I was not aware of until I placed a telephone call to your uncle, William Hurt, in Las Vegas. For, indeed, there was a current Las Vegas telephone directory in the Denver Public Library—no Walshes but one Hurt. And with great fear and trembling (literally) I called your Uncle Bill from my daughter's home in Colorado Springs.

That telephone conversation was one of the most memorable that I have ever made, as you might guess. Your uncle knew nothing of your mother's ever placing a child for adoption but said that it could have happened, for he was only 14 at the time and not too aware of all that might have occurred in his sister's life. Still, he confirmed some of the facts—her being in Denver at that time, her age, and her being married "right out of high school." The glaring discrepancy was, of course that she was married, not to Harry Walsh but to Harry Wells.

I have since consulted with genealogy experts who assure me that "glaring errors" of the sort I've mentioned are not uncommon, particularly if the certificate was copied by some clerk, perhaps days after the fact.

Of course, the most startling fact relayed to me by your uncle was that Elizabeth (Betty) Wells was still living. I was as careful and yet insistent as I could possibly be. Did he think his sister would be upset, traumatically upset, if I wrote to her? I believe that I asked him this question three times in the course of the conversation, and in every instance he assured me that, in his opinion, she would not mind. (I might add that at that point, he did not inform me that her second husband, Mr. Logue, [*sic*] had died quite recently, although he did mention him and told me of his death.)

Well, you can imagine how I sweated out **that** letter. I had absolutely **no** idea how your mother would react. The last thing I wanted was to distress her by bringing up memories that she might very well have buried for sixty years. But, as I told her, I wanted medical history at least; then, if she were willing, I would share something of my life's story with her (pictures, etc.); finally, if she wished (and only if she wished it) I would like to meet her.

Your mother never replied to my letter. At first my wife and I were sure that she would be so excited (for want of a better word) to discover that the baby had lived and had had a good life, that she would write immediately. After three months we realized, much to our disappointment, that very likely I would not hear from her.

Then began a several-month period of conjecture. Why? Why, when their other children had been kept and reared by them had they given up their first child? Of course there were all the obvious scenarios. You surely can imagine these. My own theory is that in 1925 to become pregnant, possibly while still in high school, and in a small town, would be terribly embarrassing. So the two got married, went off to the distant big city, the child was delivered and given up. Your uncle told me that your mother and father lived in Denver about three years and then returned to San Juan Pueblo where they lived for more than thirty years.

Since August last I have talked twice more with Bill Hurt, most recently on June 18, just two days after your mother's death. He and I also have corresponded twice. I find him to be a real gentle man, one who promised to talk to his sister, Carol [*sic*], as soon as he could and **then** to your mother, but who never found the occasion, apparently, to travel to Roswell. So he never found out if your mother even received my letter and what her reaction was, or why.

He did tell me about you and your sister and brother, but I assured him that I would **never** write to any of you, so long as your mother was alive and evidently either unable or unwilling to acknowledge my existence. I thought this to be the only proper way to handle such a delicate situation.

I feel, then, no further obligation to abide by this decision. I decided to write to you, rather than to Jeanne or Sam, because you live in New Mexico, close to your uncle, who has expressed a genuine interest in meeting me. I do want to meet him and hope to do so, probably this coming August. I sincerely hope that I can meet you also.

So, feel free to talk to your uncle about this. I have sent a photograph of myself to him, and he knows some of my life history. He also told me that you have been an educator living in the Espanola area for many years, and I thought that if you want more information about who I am and what sort of a fellow I am, you might know one of my former students here at Geneva College. She is a close friend of the family as well and lives in Truchas. (She is, in fact, possibly the only person I know well who lives in New Mexico.) Her name is Mrs. Margaret Franke. If you do happen to know her, don't hesitate to approach her. I'm sure that she can characterize me as well as anyone possibly could.

I told your mother in my letter to her that I have no hidden agenda in any of this. Be assured, then, that I am not interested in anything of a monetary nature. I'm interested only in one day meeting my brothers and sister if that could be possible. My adoptive mother could not have children; consequently, I have always been an only child. It **would** be nice to have siblings for a change!

Please feel free to write or to call me.

With all good wishes,

I added my telephone number, mailed the letter and prepared again to wait out the interim, but this time I set my expectations at a minimum.

About a week later, I was working at my office when Beverly called. She was so excited that she could scarcely speak. Fifteen minutes earlier Parker Wells had received my letter and was calling to express his thrill at receiving it; furthermore, would I please call him as soon as I came home that evening. At last, everything was falling into place. Beverly assured me that there was no evident reluctance on Parker's part, but just the opposite. I could scarcely wait to get home, and when I made the call I was not disappointed.

Talking with my biological brother presented no problem. There was an unlimited range of topics that immediately sprang to mind. Furthermore, Parker proved to be extremely outgoing and friendly, a trait that I found fully confirmed when I finally met him. The chief difficulty at this point was that we had not enough time to cover the possibilities that our conversation created. He described our mother's last days in some detail. She had apparently been more ill than I had suspected, based on my uncle's report. She was extremely depressed over the death of her husband. Parker was not certain that she had ever gotten my letter. He had moved her from Roswell to a nursing home in Espanola where she died. The letter, however, was never returned; I had evidently addressed it properly. I concluded that either my mother had not seen fit to answer it or that it had been lost in transit.

One significant fact emerged from that first conversation with Parker. For several years he had known about our mother's giving up a baby for adoption. Parker had graduated from New Mexico Military Institute in Roswell; subsequently, he had entered the Army where he served in the Tank Corps and Military Intelligence from 1952 to 1960, principally in Germany. It was during this time that he needed to use his birth certificate and discovered that it stated that he was the "third born" child. Knowing that he had only an older sister, Jeanne, he asked his mother about this apparent error. It was then that she told him that the statement was, indeed, correct. She told him that years before she had given up her first-born for adoption. Parker further told me that she had on at least two occasions asked him if he would be interested in taking her to Denver so that she might find out what happened to the baby. Because she lived in the far West and seldom returned to New Mexico, she had never followed her desire. Parker could not tell me whether our sister or our brother or any of the older generation knew of the adoption.

Later, Parker described how his receiving my letter provided an astonishing uplift in his emotional life. Only days before, our mother had died. His father-in-law was also gravely ill. He was, therefore, quite depressed.

So the letter announcing the existence of the baby given up more than sixty years earlier, furthermore a biological brother who very much wanted to establish a relationship, presented an entirely new situation, one filled with hope and meaning. At the end of our conversation he insisted that Beverly and I make every effort to visit him soon. I replied that it took little persuading to get me to the West again and that this was just the opportunity I was looking for. We would plan to visit him within the next six weeks.

Shortly afterward Parker wrote, describing in more detail our mother's death, stating that the family had cremated her according to her wishes, and that the family would hold a memorial service in December when our sister, Jeanne, would be able to come from Argentina.

I decided that I should be straightforward with Parker. After consulting with Margaret Franke, I wrote to inform him that for the past several months I had employed a spy to ferret out information I desired. His reaction was not at all unpleasant. Furthermore, I discovered that upon learning of Parker's father-in-law's death, Margaret and Bill had invited Parker and his wife, Floraida, to Truches for supper. Parker described their meeting with some amusement. Apparently he had never associated the Margaret he knew at the community college with this virtual "stranger" who had invited him for supper and who then confessed that she had been carrying on a secret investigation of his background for months. Not until they met at the Franke's gift shop in Truches did the realization dawn on him. Now, at last, he knew why his friend in Espanola had been so persistently inquisitive about his father's death. When, earlier, I apologized to him about my spying, it simply hadn't registered.

*   *   *

Our summer plans were relatively fixed by the time I received Parker's invitation. First, we were to attend a Carson family reunion in Southern Illinois in late July; then drive to Minnesota to an international conference sponsored by our Church. I requested permission to miss the opening faculty conference at Geneva College set for late August, so we added three weeks in the West to the schedule. By this time I was so filled with this exciting story that I was sharing it with anyone who would listen. To my surprise no one found the account boring. Reactions varied from shocked surprise, to encouragement to pursue the venture, to cautious warnings about what I might discover. We left Minnesota in early August bound for Colorado and New Mexico, scarcely knowing what to expect. It was one thing to talk by telephone to a brother whose photograph I had seen; it would be another to meet him in the flesh. With a certain amount of anxiety we arrived at our daughter's home and prepared for our visit. I called Parker to tell him of our plans and was again encouraged by the warmth of his greeting.

We agreed to come to New Mexico in a week, meanwhile occupying our time in as many ways as possible to free our minds from the thought of the impending meeting. The day arrived and we set out. We made our way into the broad San Luis Valley whose luxuriant ranches stretched to the distant mountain ranges on all sides. Turning south at Alamosa we entered New Mexico, a state that I had passed through only twice. For us it was a strange land that we had been "exploring" through books borrowed from the college library. To think! A whole family—my family— had been living here all the years that I had lived in Kansas and vacationed in Colorado, not that far distant. What had *they* been doing while I had gone to school, and played, and climbed the mountains, and fished the mountain streams, and gone to war, preached, taught, fallen in love, married and fathered a family? Would I find their experiences to be similar enough to mine that, meeting my brother, there would be *anything* to talk about? My imagination has never lacked the ability to create fantasy. Now, I was driving south, creating the fantasy of my first meeting with my brother. We would first see one another and pause, examining our mutual ground. Then, slowly we would walk to one another and embrace. "Brother!" he would say. My reply would be as simple. Then we would look at each other with amazement and joy. As I drove I checked out the fantasy. I wasn't at all sure that it would come out that way.

"Aren't you getting excited?" Beverly asked. We were now less than fifty miles from the pueblo.

"Oh," I hesitated. "I guess so." I tried to sound nonchalant about it all.

"You know," she said, "I think I'm more excited than you are."

I explained that my numerous telephone conversations with Parker had somewhat prepared me to meet him and that every indication was that the meeting would be reasonably relaxed. "My problem right now," I said, "is that we don't have a good, up-to-date map of New Mexico. Parker gave specific directions to me, but I *would* like to see more precisely where I am going on this map to understand his instructions more clearly."

"Any place we can stop?" she asked.

We had been travelling through an especially barren stretch of New Mexico. "I haven't seen any place that might have a map," I said, "but, surely, there'll be a town soon."

There wasn't. Just two tiny gas stations that broke the long lonely stretch of highway. Neither had a map. Apparently, either the travelers on this road were thoroughly familiar with the territory or they came better prepared than I. There seemed to be no demand for road maps whatsoever.

"Just read the directions," I told her, "and hope for the best."

Parker's directions proved to be adequate, however, and soon we found ourselves crossing a bridge and entering what surely was the pueblo. I had never been in a pueblo before, but the adobe homes clustered around a public square, a Catholic church, a post office, what appeared to be one or two small business establishments, and a larger adobe building that housed a sort of museum and salesroom where one could buy crafts peculiar to the San Juan Pueblo, convinced me that we were at my brother's doorstep.

"A quarter mile down the road." Beverly was still reading from Parker's directive. "The only house with a peaked roof—and red."

Almost immediately we emerged from the pueblo. "That's got to be it," I said, looking straight ahead to a house matching the directions, fronted by huge cottonwood trees, an irrigation ditch and a wire fence. We drove into the yard, parked the car between the house and an incredibly green island of grass surrounding a small locust tree, turned off the engine and waited. This was it! What would happen now?

"Well," Beverly said, giving me that let's-face-the-music look, "we might as well get out."

"Okay," I replied. We climbed out, stretched, and decided to make for the back rather than the front door. A man and a woman made their way around the corner of the house. He had a broad grin on his face.

"Brother!" he said. "Welcome!" And almost as an afterthought, "After all these years!"

Parker's wife, Floraida, added significantly, "Parker and I saw you get out of the car and we said, almost together, 'He looks just like Uncle Bill!'"

My fantasy did not fully correspond with reality, but one thing did. Our embrace was strong and real. No tears. We simply held on and savored the moment.

Meanwhile, Floraida welcomed Beverly. She was a quiet, soft-spoken, attractive Hispanic woman. Having made our greetings, we went into the house. Eventually, Parker told me something of the history of the place. At the moment he was the only Anglo living within the pueblo. The property belonged originally to a Spanish family, and by the terms of the 1848 Treaty of Guadeloupe-Hidalgo, such property was to be held in perpetuity by the original Spanish owners and their descendants, even though the Pueblo Indians were permanently settled on the land that was declared to be theirs. Eventually, Parker explained, our father had bought this parcel of land from the Spanish descendants in the autumn of 1930 and had agreed to deed half of its nearly four acres to the pueblo. I reminded myself several times that first night that this was the house where I could have spent my childhood had I remained in the family. I soon discovered that Parker was what one sometimes called "handy," that is, he had a natural talent for carpentry and had, over a period of years, continually remodeled and added to the house. It no longer resembled the house that our parents had moved into back in the 1930s. The central core was still there, but Parker's accretions had changed its appearance considerably.

The house struck us as a kind of oasis set amid the dusty fields of the area. The sixty-foot cottonwoods offered shelter from the worst of the New Mexico sun. Parker had learned the art of adobe wall construction, so the immediate property lay within a three-foot wall that entirely enclosed his lawn and gardens. Along the north wall he had laid out a rose garden, the last thing I had expected in that country. The roses were extraordinary! They stood tall, with their large, fragrant blossoms in the full second bloom of the season. Protected from the severity of the winter—this was not truly desert country—their enormous stems gave proof of their vigor. Beverly later remarked that she was impressed that both brothers had such an interest in gardening, particularly in raising roses. I admitted that, although I had some pride in my rose culture, what Parker had produced astounded me. The lawn was immaculate, as lush as the tiny bit I had noticed upon my arrival. Not a weed in sight! The trees and vines within the compound and the garden on the south side of the house likewise gave evidence of Parker and Floraida's great love of gardening. Parker had enclosed in glass the original patio along the south wall of the house creating a splendid room in which to feast or relax. This solarium was not only a marvel in the summertime but also functioned beautifully as a source of heat in the winter when the December sun worked its magic there. Parker had converted the original garage into a workshop, and one could stand behind the shop and gaze eastward across the broad plain of the Northern Rio Grande Valley to the Sangre de Christo range and west to Santa Clara Mountain. We were just beginning to understand the meaning of the New Mexico state motto—"Land of Enchantment."

*　　　*　　　*

Any misgivings that we might have had about how the initial moments would develop were soon dispelled. Parker proved to be every bit as outgoing in the flesh as he had been in our earlier conversations. Floraida, in her own quiet way, exercised her hospitality, providing a welcome lunch, and, later, at suppertime, a taste of wonderful Hispanic cooking. She gradually became more and more involved in the conversation, for she had a natural ability to pick up as much of the family history as Parker could relate to her. Occasionally, she would correct Parker on a point. Parker would usually admit his error with good grace. It was evident to us that they were deeply in love. The four of us spent our next twelve hours, almost continuously talking "family." Parker had set out in the living room boxes of photos and numerous photograph albums that provided the basis for the "history lesson" that Parker began to teach me.

Gradually, through these photographs, a picture of my mother and father emerged. There were many more pictures of her than of him, for I learned that our father had suffered a fall as a young child, the exact cause of which was shrouded in mystery. Among the various accounts, the most pervasive was that someone had pushed him, accidentally or otherwise, down a long flight of steps that led from the second-story balcony to the ground at the rear of his Las Vegas home. The fall had caused severe and permanent damage to his spine, so that at maturity he stood only slightly over five feet. The fall also gave him an unnatural stoop that he spent his whole life compensating for by standing in a particularly erect position, throwing out his chest in an unusual manner. His two sisters, Louise and Nellie, took particular interest in protecting him in his childhood. They called him "brother" a name that early on became "buzzy" instead. Harry Wells, throughout his life, was known, then, to most of his acquaintances as "Buzzy" Wells.

Apparently, as a young man our father became somewhat notorious, for "Buzzy" became known in Las Vegas for his feisty nature and his generally "macho" demeanor. He was never comfortable, however, to have his photograph taken. Very few pictures of my father exist.

The same cannot be said for my mother. The boxes and albums contained dozens of pictures of her, from the time she was a tiny child, beautifully dressed and crowned with blonde ringlets until she reached her late seventies, still a tiny woman whose weathered face carried intriguing aspects of character that I could only guess at. As I sat on Parker's sofa with the photos spread out between us, on our laps or on the floor, I could not help wondering why I had not had the chance to meet her just once. Why had God taken her just at the time I finally came to know of her existence? My regret was almost overwhelming, but, trusting in the providence of a sovereign God, whose ways are past our ways, my regret gradually disappeared. I eventually became resigned to the fact that, close as it had been, I was never to know her; therefore, I determined to discover as much as I could *about* her. Parker and Floraida would help me there; eventually, others in the family would bring their insights to bear on that learning process as well.

The number of albums that chronicled our mother's last twenty-five years following her marriage to Gomer Lague particularly impressed me. An album, filled with pictures of Tahiti, told of her trip with Gomer who was consulting with the agriculture interests in the island. Other albums depicted visits to Europe, across the United States and elsewhere. There were photographs showing her holding up a prize salmon catch from a fishing trip on Puget Sound and photographs of her home in Gig Harbor.

I learned about her difficult life during the thirties when the mercantile business wasn't doing well. The effects of the Great Depression were obvious. The forties, when our father and his partners bought out Ruth and Kramer Mercantile, showed little improvement. One of the partners failed to hold up his end of the business; there was too much money out "on the street." Our mother, who had been an extraordinary business student in high school, had taken a job with the New Mexico Department of Welfare and had worked long hours, first in Santa Fe, then in Espanola. That was her way to make ends meet. Much of our parents' life included socializing with a group of friends whom Buzzy had cultivated in his job. Gomer was one of those who had grown to know our father and mother well, both in his capacity as a flour salesman and as our father's close companion. Within a year of our father's death in 1963, Gomer, by then divorced, had proposed to Betty, and she had accepted. From all accounts, her life on the West Coast with Gomer had been a happy one; her interests fitted Gomer's well. For the first time in years she knew no financial distress.

I was able to guess much of this history from the pictures that Parker was now showing me. I found myself studying them intently. I noted how much my mother changed in appearance, often from one year to the next. She would put on weight; then take it off, each change altering her appearance. I compared the picture taken of her as a high school girl—a "flapper" with bobbed blonde hair, slim and tiny, and the picture taken with the prize fish, years later, still tiny, but so very changed. The years had taken their toll. Still, despite it all, there was so much character in that face that I was certain that she would have been a fascinating woman to have known.

Gradually, the stack of photos disappeared into their boxes. Our wives began to question us about our habits, our preferences, those peculiarities we demonstrated and which they had come to know so well. What were our interests? Were there things that demonstrated strong resemblance between us? Some of the questions dealt with substantive matters; others were simply silly.

"Parker," Beverly asked, "how do *you* put the roll of toilet paper on the dispenser, rolling out from the front or down from the rear?"

Floraida: "Do you insist, Norman, on planning every trip, down to the tiniest detail—time of departure, time of arrival, miles to go, and so forth?"

"While we're at it," Parker added in mock seriousness, "do you generally cross your right leg over your left or vice versa?"

"Even more significant," Beverly broke in, before I could answer his question, "can you wrap one leg completely around the other?"

Parker tried and failed. We *weren't* exactly clones, after all.

We found, however, that in many respects there were strong like-nesses—our similar wide-ranging interests, our love of music, of the arts, of nature, our attention to detail. Interestingly enough, there were marked differences as well. Although we had musical tastes that were similar, Parker was not an especially gifted singer. I had managed to learn most of the skills used in building or maintaining a home, but Parker was much more the natural craftsman. Parker loved to read, but his intellectual interests and abilities lay more in the mathematical than in the verbal side. Each of us had an intense interest in sports, but Parker was a more naturally gifted athlete than I had ever been. Beverly remarked later how much more outgoing Parker was than I, and I had to admit that walking right up to a stranger and striking up a conversation, something which Parker would constantly do, was certainly not my forte.

Floraida's special dinner interrupted that first long acquaintance session, and now I met for the first time a member of the older generation—my father's older sister, Louise—and a member of the younger generation, Parker's son, Ken. Aunt Louise lived in a nearby nursing home where Parker and Floraida could look after her. She had lived with them for some time following an apparently unnecessary operation on her knees that rendered her incapable of walking. She lived, therefore, in her bed and her wheelchair. Parker invited me to accompany him to pick her up and bring her to dinner. From the beginning, Beverly and I found Aunt Louise a delight! A tall, handsome woman with salt-and-pepper hair, she possessed a keen mind and winsome sense of humor. She had never married. We discovered later that her single status had not occurred for lack of suitors. I gravitated to her naturally, partly because she, like Parker and Floraida, extended a warmth of acceptance, and partly because she told me that she had both taught high school English and had been a school administrator for forty-three years, primarily in Albuquerque. Ah! I thought, here's a woman after my own heart!

The dinnertime conversation, probably to Ken's consternation, continued from that of the afternoon—further family history. This time, I learned much more about my father's side of the family, for Louise's memory was sharp, her story telling fascinating. For the first time in my life I learned that, contrary to what I had always assumed, I had other than Scotch-Irish blood in my veins. My paternal grandmother, Lena Henrietta Hess, was German. Although this fact did not floor me, I found myself mulling it over in my mind, especially as I began to learn more about my grandmother. Her mother had divorced her father and remarried. In 1881 Lena and her brother, George, came to Las Vegas, New Mexico, from Newton, Kansas, with her stepfather, Caleb Preston. There were three younger Preston children. Lena Henrietta Hess had married Samuel Harris Wells and for about two years lived in Clayton, New Mexico, where they managed a hotel. Eventually they returned to Las Vegas where their three children were born. Here, she managed the Plaza Hotel in West Las Vegas, familiarly known as Old Town. Lena herself purchased the land on which they built a fine Queen Anne Victorian, two-story brick home with a wrap around veranda in East Las Vegas, or New Town. Their home was a short distance from that of the Hurts, who dwelt in a very comfortable but modest duplex.

Few photos remained of Grandmother Wells, but all attested to her character. Ramrod straight, tall and of serious demeanor, Grandmother Wells was a force to be reckoned with. Formal photographs of that era seldom reveal anything about the fun-loving side of people. Apparently, however, the pictures of my grandmother did not lie. She was evidently so stern that some persons, half seriously, called her "the witch." It would seem that she was the dominant force in the family; eventually she and Grandfather grew apart, and one day he left her. This situation, so common today, caused a scandal then. Grandmother characteristically took things into her own hands, divorced Grandfather, and henceforth effectively erased him from the life of the family. He eventually turned up again, having remarried and fathered a son.

Grandmother was now on her own, but the owners of the hotel offered her the opportunity to continue to manage it. Thus she was able to provide a more than adequate income for her and the children. Later, I would discover what lay behind the offer.

*   *   *

Of course, one twelve-hour running conversation, complete with visual aids, cannot begin to compensate for a gap of more than sixty years in one's life. It was a beginning, however, for it was the first opening into my life of the lives of an entirely other family. It could have been distressing but proved not to be. For now, as Beverly pointed out, we shared in a third family, something few couples experience. As the days passed, we found a whole new world opening up to us, the world of the American Southwest, with its Hispanic and Native American cultures. Visits with Parker and Floraida to the Indian market in Santa Fe, introductions to the many Native Americans in the pueblo with whom Parker had grown up; trips to Los Alamos, Albuquerque, the O'Keefe home in Abiquiu; treks to Chimayo, Truchas or Taos to the north and east; watching the long, slow dying of the sun behind Santa Clara Peak; and traveling through the spectacular canyons to the northwest that have fascinated many artists and writers through the years, flaming rock walls standing silently beneath the brilliant blue of the New Mexico sky.

My brother's evident warmth and receptivity made him the ideal person to introduce me to as many family members as he could. We continued our visits with Aunt Louise, gleaning valuable information, coming to recognize her wit, intelligence and charm. Despite the charm, however, an unsettling note entered our conversation.

On one occasion when I was absent, Aunt Louise firmly asserted to Beverly that, while she found me to be a fine man and an honest searcher, I was not her nephew.

It became apparent that my mother's hasty marriage had occurred under a cloud; so Aunt Louise naturally questioned my paternity. Although she and others of her generation were apparently suspicious about a baby who might have been born in Denver and then given away, no one had pursued the matter through the years. If a child had indeed been born, the matter of its paternity created a strong difference of opinion between the two families; the Hurts believing that Buzzy Wells was the father; the Wells just as vigorously denying it. For my part, that I might very well have been conceived out of wedlock was no real surprise. I had come to expect just such a fact. Under the circumstances, Aunt Louise's opinion that I was not her brother's child was also understandable. I determined to put the best face on the situation and "accept" Aunt Louise as *my* aunt despite the element of doubt.

A day or two later, in Santa Fe, we finally met Uncle Bill Hurt, the man who was my first contact with the family. I had always had some difficulty seeing the resemblance others saw between Parker and me. Perhaps I did not see myself physically as clearly as one might expect. When Uncle Bill walked through the door of the cafeteria where we were to meet, I again had something of the same reaction, but none of the others, except perhaps his wife, Katie, shared that feeling. Katie, for reasons known only to her, admitted that Bill and I looked "a tiny bit alike—perhaps." There followed another lengthy mealtime conversation at which time I saw more of the character of my mother's brother. He proved to be as soft spoken as I had found him in our earlier telephone conversations.

A gentle person, he had spent his adult life in the Las Vegas public school system, retiring as Assistant Superintendent. I later discovered how respected he was among his colleagues and students. I had learned of Parker's interest in painting; he had shown me a couple of examples of his work; now I learned that Uncle Bill was an accomplished pen-and-ink artist, someone who could always be counted on to produce a sketch for special occasions: a reproduction of his church building to enhance the stationery sold by the ladies' guild, Christmas and birthday cards for the family. For years I had a secret desire to paint, but I had never carried it out. Could it be, I thought, that down there in the depth of my psyche lurked some potential artistic talent? It was evidently there in *some* members of the family at least!

Both Bill and Katie were active members of the local Methodist church; Katie was the daughter of a Methodist pastor, and, as most Methodist preacher's kids who grew up early in this century, had lived in numerous small towns in Nebraska where her father served in a variety of pastorates. There was a twinkle in Katie's eye. Was it a remnant of a mischievous spirit born in earlier days on the plains or was it simple good humor? Possibly a bit of both. Aunt Katie had what some might call "an independent nature," frank and direct. She spoke her piece, but never harshly, always with a soupcon of humor. Both she and Uncle Bill loved to play golf; however, it was evident that she scarcely shared his enthusiasm for genealogy.

A few days later we spent some time with them in Las Vegas, and I was able to see where both families had grown up. Uncle Bill willingly took me all around the town, which has its own exciting history growing out of its connection with the railroad, the cattle trails, and the colorful life of the early West, with its own brand of morality and justice. We made our way to the Masonic cemetery at the edge of town to see the graves of my Grandfather and Grandmother Hurt. Katie accompanied us, somewhat reluctantly I thought, and remarked about how much less carefully they were keeping the cemetery than in years past. Parker furthered my acquaintance with Las Vegas by lending me books from his and Aunt Louise's collection that described the town in its more triumphant if less conventional days. They told me that the creative gift extended to Uncle Bill's family; that my cousin, Marcia, a rancher's wife living in Eastern New Mexico, was an author of popular romances, albeit under a pseudonym, and by that means added a significant amount to the family income. As her mother described her daughter's accomplishments, I mentally gave Marcia great credit. "She really has her heart set on a better sort of literature," Katie confided.

I'm sure, I thought, she'll make it, given her determination and drive. Again the fact confronted me that here in the family there existed genuine creative ability

Weeks before, in an early telephone conversation, Uncle Bill had told me of the Hurt migration to the West. My Great Grandfather Hurt had come to New Mexico for reasons of health. Apparently he suffered from some serious illness and had been advised to "go West" from his native Tennessee shortly after the Civil War, in which he had fought with distinction.

Having been engaged in coal mining in Alabama following the Civil War, he had settled first in Los Cerrillos, New Mexico, where he was employed as a company store owner by a coal mining firm operated since 1853 by Abraham Staab. Grandfather Hurt started working at age fourteen. His job was to carry the receipts each night by horseback from Cerrillos to Madrid, ten miles distant and the location of the nearest bank. Eventually he began to work for the railroad itself, finally becoming a conductor.

No forbear in my adoptive family was anything but Northern; Mother Carson's family had moved from South Carolina to Illinois because they refused to hold slaves. Never, even in my wildest imagination, had I considered the possibility of my being connected with the South, and now, I discovered that, at least on the Hurt side of the family, I had Rebel ancestry! Furthermore, I discovered that the connection with the South remains to this day, that one branch of the family still lives in Atlanta. The horizons of my family were constantly expanding in the most extraordinary way.

Also my predisposition to think less highly of athletic skill than I ought was being challenged. For not only had Uncle Bill been a better than average athlete in his youth, but he brought to my attention in the form of a faded newspaper clipping one of his favorite pieces of family history. It seems that my grandmother's brother from southern Kansas, one Charles "Dusty" Rhodes, had been a successful pitcher for the St. Louis Cardinals, having pitched briefly in 1908 and then brought up again from Omaha in 1909. The clipping, dated Sunday, April 18, 1909, describes Rhodes' 4-1 victory over the world champion Chicago Cubs, with its famous combination of Tinker, Evers and Chance. Unfortunately he burned out his arm "on a cold day" a few years later and had to retire from the sport. These discoveries produced even more mystery. If there *were* genetic reasons for my proclivity for the arts—my great aunt, Mary Hurt Van Stone, had been an accomplished pianist in Santa Fe and a friend of Aaron Copland—why so obvious a failure to connect in the realm of athletic ability? I dismissed the thought from my mind.

*   *   *

Between the visit with Parker and the visit with Uncle Bill and Aunt Katie we took our longest side trip and met a very important member of the family. Having called her in advance, we made our way one week end to Roswell to meet my mother's sister, Margaret Carroll Patterson. Long ago Carroll and Betty had sworn to one another that, should they become widows, left to fend for themselves, they would make every effort to spend their last days together. And so it had transpired. Aunt Carroll had been a widow for three years when Gomer Lague died; now both were widows. Though my mother was in poor health and somewhat reluctant to leave the cool climate of the Pacific Northwest, the family thought it best to bring her to New Mexico where they could care for her more easily. Eventually, she came to live with Carroll, and of course, this is where she had been living when I wrote my letter the year before. Here she suffered her most debilitating stroke that eventually took her life.

The trip to Roswell took us into another New Mexico, an area not of mountain scenery but of a desert, marked by oil wells and relieved by cotton fields that flourished because of the artesian wells found there. We had thought northern New Mexico relatively pleasant (it was unusually cool that year), but we began to discover the heat of the desert as we dropped down out of the central mountain ranges and made our way across the vast stretches of southeastern New Mexico. We arrived in Roswell in late afternoon, and, despite our happy meeting with Parker, we found ourselves curiously tense as we drove up to Aunt Carroll's house.

"I thought I'd get over this nervousness by now," I remarked as I rang the doorbell.

"Well, you know," Beverly said, "even though it's family, we're meeting another stranger, really."

I had no time to reply. The door opened only partially and we were greeted by a tiny woman who peered up at me somewhat quizzically.

"Mrs. Patterson?" I had decided that I would begin by being formal.

"Yes," she said, "are you Norman?"

"I am," I replied. "But I guess I really wasn't quite prepared to call you Aunt Carroll."

A trace of a smile crossed her face. "Come in," she said.

We entered her handsome ranch style home. Funny, I thought, how I had imagined this house in Roswell would look when I sent that letter last year. I had imagined a two-story frame house circa 1915, with a veranda—a house much more like the old Wells homestead in Las Vegas. How totally my imagination had let me down!

We followed Aunt Carroll into her immaculate home. Everything in its place. The furniture, carpets, pictures, curtains—all in good taste. The conversation started much more slowly than it had with Parker. Instead of a rush of information, we began a slow, almost painful step-by-careful-step dialogue for the first half hour. Later, Aunt Carroll told me that she had been every bit as apprehensive as I had been. Here, on her doorstep was the author of that astonishing letter sent to her sister the year before, someone whom she had never seen. Despite the earnest tone of that letter, could she trust him? Was he after something? Was there some ulterior motive in all this?

Gradually the conversation warmed; the reserve all of us felt began to ebb. I asked about her family, about her own background. She had never gotten far from the railroad background of the Hurt family. Her husband,

Marc "Pat" Patterson, who had died in 1984, worked for the Santa Fe, eventually becoming the private secretary for the regional director of the line. He too, I discovered, was a compulsively meticulous person. There was one son, Paul, who had spent most of his adult life as a rancher. Except for the few months that my mother lived with her, Carroll had lived alone since her husband's death. Inevitably the conversation turned to the subject that consumed me.

"Then my mother *did* receive my letter."

"Yes," my aunt replied, "and she took it straight off to her bedroom and read it." She added that Betty had not come out then for some time.

"Aunt Carroll," I asked, "what was her reaction? I'm really curious."

"You have to remember," she said, "that Betty was not at all well. Not only did her strokes affect her physically but also mentally. She was right as rain most of the time but could become confused at times. For example, she had trouble making decisions."

"This was one of the possibilities we had thought of. It was very disappointing to us—and strange—that I never received a reply from her. I just couldn't figure it out."

Aunt Carroll grew serious. "I must tell you," she said, "that she was deeply touched by the letter. There is absolutely no question about that. Yet," she added, "I found her also to be very unsure of herself about answering it."

I waited. Aunt Carroll continued. "I would ask Betty, 'Don't you want to answer his letter? Don't you really think you owe it to him?' She would say, 'yes,' and then by the next day have either forgotten the conversation or have decided against writing. I never did completely convince her. You see, she really couldn't write any longer."

"Yes, I understand. Maybe it's for the best."

"I really think so," she said. "I hate to think of your seeing her like that." Aunt Carroll paused, her face darkening. "She just wasn't the same old Betty anymore, full of life, of sparkle, you know." She continued, "I told her that I would type the letter for her. Even that didn't work." She looked intently at me again and smiled. "But, Norman, she died happy—happy in the knowledge that you were alive after all and that you had been well-taken care of and that you had made something of yourself."

I knew at that instant that I had made the right decision by writing the letter. Although I was never to see my biological mother, missing that opportunity by a mere fraction of the time that I had had no knowledge of her, I was overwhelmed by great joy in realizing that she had finally reached closure and that I had provided some measure of comfort and peace to her in her last days.

The following day was a Sunday, and Carroll suggested that we attend a Southern Baptist Church close by. The service was enthusiastic and warm, filled with the Spirit. The minister gave the usual invitation for all guests to rise and identify themselves, and I did so, feeling a genuine sense of blood relationship with this tiny woman seated beside me in the pew. As we left the church, Aunt Carroll, who knew the minister even though she ordinarily worshipped at a nearby Methodist church, introduced me. As we walked away from the church, down the hot Roswell sidewalk, she paused and took my hand. Looking up at me she asked, "Did you hear what I said to the minister?"

I had to admit that I had been concentrating on catching his name at that moment. "No, I guess I didn't notice. I'm sorry."

"I introduced you as 'my nephew, Norman,'" she said, smiling, and she squeezed my arm. "You are, you know," she added, "and I like the idea."

The more we came to know Aunt Carroll that day, the more we too liked the idea. We learned more about the family. How Uncle "Pat" had played in a little dance band for years, about his arrowhead collection, about her son Paul's interest in writing about the West. I decided to address one further subject that I considered to be very touchy. Otherwise, I would never be completely satisfied. I decided to bring up the paternity question that had plagued the relationship between the two families. I felt that I now knew Aunt Carroll well enough to broach the subject without embarrassing either of us.

"Well, *I'm* convinced that Harry was your father," Aunt Carroll said. "Betty had been seeing him for some time," she continued. "When she realized that she was pregnant, she called him immediately. From everything that she told me—and you must realize that we were *very* close—I'm convinced that he was the father."

Then Aunt Carroll told us about the events of those few days in 1924. Buzzy had readily agreed to marry Betty and proposed that he go up to Denver immediately following the marriage to look for work and a place to live. The marriage took place in the living room of the Presbyterian manse, September 4, 1924, without the knowledge of either family. Carroll and a friend stood up with the couple. Harry left the next morning for Denver, and the two sisters, thinking to hide the marriage, boarded a train bound for Kansas City for a two-week visit with an uncle who lived there. It might have worked as they planned, except that the court reporter for the local newspaper published, as was his custom, the record of marriage license applications. The sisters had scarcely arrived in Kansas City before both families knew the truth. When Betty and Carroll returned to Las Vegas they found themselves the victims of the wrath of both families. Neither family took action to annul the marriage, and Betty left for Denver. The feeling generated by the marriage had become transformed, however, into a degree of denial. I might indeed be a Hurt, but I was surely not a Wells.

"We *did* do the wrong thing," Aunt Carroll smiled ruefully, "but it's so long ago now. I regretted it at the time," she said, "but gradually I've put it out of mind. As far as I'm concerned," she repeated firmly, "Harry Wells is your father."

At this point we dropped the subject.

It was hard to leave Aunt Carroll, for by now all the hesitation and reserve had been replaced by acceptance and loving concern. However, part we did, making our way northward to Las Vegas and our visit with Uncle Bill; then back to Colorado Springs. A whole new world had opened up to us, not simply the enchanted land of New Mexico, but the fascinating realm of a new and exciting family. I now possessed three interesting and wonderful families, my adoptive family, my wife's family, and my biological family. Here was something I felt that I could treasure, something I knew not all adopted children could claim. And I rejoiced.

Las Vegas girls basketball team, 1922-23
Betty Hurt, second from left

2417 W. 32nd Street, Denver, Colo.
Maternity Hospital, 1989

2200 Champa, Denver, Colo.
Boarding house, 1989

Harry "Buzzy" Wells, Betty H. Wells

Margaret Carroll Patterson, Betty (Wells) Lague,
Robert Kemper Hurt, William Hurt

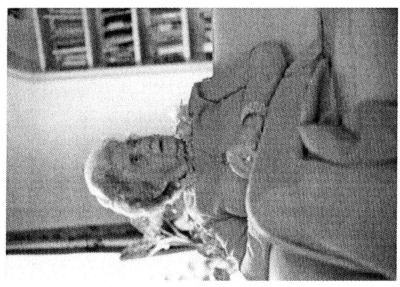

Nellie Hernandez, 1975

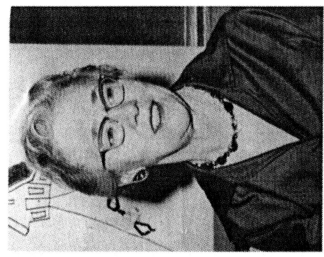

Louise Wells, 1957

Jeanne W. Keating

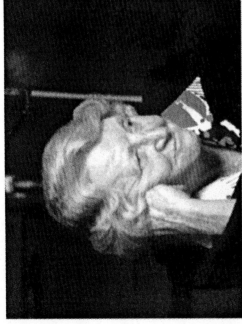

Betty (Wells) Lague, 1982

Parker Wells, Norman Carson, Jeanne Keating, Samuel Wells, 1988

Parker Wells, Norman Carson, 1988

4

Rethinking My Heritage

It was now time to return to Pennsylvania and the new academic year. As we drove east from New Mexico, Beverly and I discussed the implications of all that had happened over the previous fifteen months. Despite the concentration of events that had occurred within the past few days, there was much about my new family that I had not yet discovered. I had met neither my youngest brother, Sam, nor my sister, Jeanne. Nor had I met many of my cousins. I was curious about these family members, particularly about how they would respond to me. I tried to imagine how they would react to a stranger who had come into their life, announcing that he was a brother or a cousin they had never heard of.

Would they resent my intrusion into their lives? Would they suspect that somehow this easterner carried sinister ulterior motives? Would they simply ignore me, clearly indicating that my existence aroused not a whit of curiosity nor interest? On the basis of my experience with Parker, Uncle Bill, Aunt Katie, and Aunt Carroll, I was confident that things *might* turn out favorably, for those I had already met had certainly welcomed me warmly; perhaps the rest of the family would do the same.

The first test of my assumption came quickly. My brother, Sam, lived in Miami, Oklahoma, a town located not far off the direct route to Pennsylvania. So, from Colorado Springs we drove across southern Kansas, for I wanted to see where my grandmother Rhodes' family had lived before she moved to New Mexico. Although I had lived for sixteen years in central Kansas, I had never been to Montgomery County in the southeast corner of the state. Uncle Bill had written that the Rhodes family lived on the farm near Caney, a small town almost astride the Kansas-Oklahoma line. We had just enough time to visit the local cemetery. It took little time to find the stone marking my great-grandmother's grave: *Ida Rhodes, born 1864, died 1918.* Uncle Bill had also written that she had died of the Spanish influenza, cut down, as were so many thousands, by that dreadful plague. A thought crossed my mind. What if my Aunt Grace, nursing flu victims in New Mexico, had actually cared for my great-grandmother? It was not beyond the realm of possibility. We left the cemetery and drove to Joplin, Missouri, where by prior arrangement we were to meet Sam and his family.

After checking into the motel, we went to the lobby where we had agreed to meet them. As we sat there, watching various families enter, I again found myself getting nervous. Would it be particularly difficult to recognize Sam? We had no clear idea of what Sam looked like. How would he recognize me? Perhaps we really hadn't communicated clearly enough. The prospect of sizing up an unknown brother in the crowded lobby of the motel was daunting, like evaluating a prospective blind date before the actual meeting. Would he appear alone? We thought that we had been told he would bring his family with him, but we had no idea how many family members would appear. After several tense moments, a family of five entered. They walked past us once and circled around the room. Was it possible that this was Sam and his family? They returned. The father approached and spoke.

"Are you Norman?" He offered his hand.

I took it in mine. "Yes, I am," I answered.

My reply produced an immediate look of relief on everyone's face. We made introductions all around. Sam, the youngest child in the family, was smaller than Parker and I. Speaking in his rather high-pitched voice, he expressed his delight in meeting me and Beverly and introduced his wife, Dixie, and the three children who accompanied him: his eldest,

Sammy III, Ben, and Sarah Louise. Sam told us that a fourth child, Tim, lived in Oregon.

Later, over supper in a nearby Chinese restaurant, we replicated our first visit with Parker by filling in as many details about our personal lives as time would allow. Sam, a graduate of Eastern New Mexico State in Portales, was a geology teacher in Northeastern Oklahoma A & M. In addition, he coached men's soccer. Sam said that, being the youngest member of the family, nine years younger than his sister, Jeanne, he had never had a close relationship with her. He was, however, closer to Parker. He had married Dixie, a girl who lived near San Juan Pueblo, when they were both quite young. By this time Dixie entered fully into the conversation. She had not had the opportunity to receive much formal education beyond high school; nevertheless, she was an intelligent woman with an infectious laugh that demonstrated a generally happy disposition.

Sammy and Ben took part as well, chatting about their varied interests, particularly that of participating for a number of years in drum and bugle corps bands. They and Tim had been members of several such bands, performing in contests in various parts of the United States. Sarah Louise, the youngest child, was still in high school and intent on pursuing her education further. As I sat across the table from her I noticed that she was particularly interested in studying my face. My curiosity aroused, I was going to ask about this when she spoke.

"I can't believe it," she said, "but when I look at your mouth and chin, I see my grandmother. And as you talk, I see her even more clearly."

"Well, you're not the first to see a family resemblance. You know, I find that somehow quite satisfying."

"I'm glad you do. It's a thrill for me to meet you."

Our conversation continued in this vein for some time over the meal, but eventually Sam and his family had to return to Miami. Beverly and I returned to our room and, after comparing observations as we lay in bed, fell asleep. One more member of the family accounted for, and again no repercussions, no regrets, and scarcely a hint of strain or awkwardness. To my delight my family was turning out to be both fascinating and delightful.

*   *   *

Throughout the month I continued to build a relationship with Parker and Floraida, and in early September he informed me that Jeanne would be able to fly to the United States in December; therefore, he had set the date for our mother's memorial service to take place then. To my astonishment he insisted that Beverly and I come to the service. Parker had chosen the chapel of the McCurdy School, a private Methodist school in Espanola. Parker had attended McCurdy before transferring to New Mexico Military Institute, and both of his sons, Dean and Ken, had graduated there, so Parker was on friendly terms with the administration. Beverly and I needed little time to make our decision; although it might be somewhat awkward for everyone when I presented myself as the unknown son, it was, more importantly, a natural opportunity for me to meet more members of the family.

So it was that, for the second time that year, we arrived in New Mexico. Parker and Floraida met us at the Albuquerque airport where we awaited my sister's arrival from Argentina. Having discovered that Jeanne's flight had already arrived, the four of us began to search for her. The airport, however, was undergoing extensive renovations; because various passageways were closed, we found ourselves wandering through narrow alleys between plywood walls. The more we wandered the more frustrated we became. We were not alone in our frustration, for shortly we passed a woman sitting on her suitcase in what seemed to be a state of near exhaustion. Because Parker passed by her, I paid little attention.

Parker stopped, however, and looking back, recognized his sister. When Jeanne arrived she made a valiant effort to find where she should go to meet Parker. Exhausted, she had set her suitcase down and was now sitting on it in utter frustration while she gathered her strength to continue her search. Parker approached her and, after a quick hug, turned to me and introduced us. Finally, I had met each of my biological siblings. There was little need for extended conversation at this point, for all were weary from travel, Jeanne most of all. We made our way to Parker's car and began our return journey to Espanola.

I had seen photographs of Jeanne—three years my junior—one, when she was a university student and another as a mother of two children, a daughter and a son. The photographs, however, had not fully prepared me for the present reality. She was quite petite, almost tiny. Although my mother was a small woman, somehow I had not expected it in her daughter. While she was considerably older than when the photographs were taken, she retained her classic features. She was no longer the blonde college student with bobbed hair, yet she was still an attractive woman. Over the next three days, I came to learn much more about her.

Our father had obviously favored her as a child, and, as I gathered in the few conversations I had with her, she fully reciprocated this feeling. The following year, Jeanne wrote to me, describing our father as she saw him:

> He was a darling, clever fellow…I do remember the sparkle in
> his eye, a sweet smile and joy in life. He loved San Juan and the
> Indians, the outdoors and wildlife. He was intelligent and sensi-
> tive. I think the stress of making ends meet drove him to drink.
> Anyway, I learned to swim, ride, shoot, fish, dance and lots of
> things from him.

Jeanne loved her mother too, but I could sense that over the years there had developed a distance between them. Her fondest memories were of her father. Her parents had given her the advantage of a university education, where she majored in Spanish. At some point she had learned to play golf, becoming skilled enough to win the Punta del Este, Uruguay, championship a record eleven times.

As she pursued her education at the university, she found that the pueblo and the Espanola valley, as it was often called, held no attraction for her. She once remarked that she had one goal—to leave the valley permanently. She had greater things in mind: perhaps golfing fame, certainly the monetary benefits to be gained by her university degree, almost certainly the opportunity to marry well and enjoy the comfortable life. Following graduation, she took her skills to Washington, D. C. where she worked for the State Department, a career that took her eventually to South America where she was employed by the U. S. embassy in Buenos Aires.

There she met Lawrence Keating whom she married in 1951. Keating, fifteen years Jeanne's senior, was a native of New England who worked as a textile engineer for Boston-based United Merchants Manufacturing Co. Sudamtex, the company branch in South America, was the first to produce polyester on that continent. Jeanne was Lawrence's second wife and bore him two children, Patricia and William. Jeanne Keating had never again to worry about a comfortable life. The couple had a home in Buenos Aires and a summer villa in Puenta del Este. They moved in the best circles. Jeanne had everything she might want and was contented and happy, far from life in New Mexico. Their life, however, was not totally trouble free. In 1958 they suffered a serious auto accident from which Lawrence never completely recovered. In 1968, he died of a heart attack.

Fortunately, a trust fund established in the United States enabled Jeanne to live almost as comfortably as before. She made some economic adjustments—sold their boat—and she settled down to a future in Argentina. Patricia married Santiago Cavanagh, a local farmer of Irish descent. William, however, suffered from epileptic seizures; eventually, Jeanne took him to Seattle where he underwent surgery at the University of Washington Medical Center that corrected the condition. He continues to live there. When I finally met my sister, she had been widowed for twenty years and was well acquainted with both the pleasures and the tragedies of life.

*　　　　　*　　　　　*

Our mother's memorial service took place on December 11, 1988, in the McCurdy Chapel. The chapel was filled. There were many from the area who remembered Betty Wells from earlier years when she had worked as a secretary for the New Mexico Department of Human Service. Some were Hispanics who remembered her happy disposition when she attended to their needs. Others were San Juan Indians who had known her and our father during the years when he dealt with them in the store. Parker was in charge of the simple, brief service. For me, the most touching moment came when he asked me and Beverly to stand and announced to his many friends that I was his brother, Betty's eldest child, adding a brief but necessary explanation for my absence through all those years.

Following the service the closest friends and the family gathered for a luncheon at nearby Rancho de Chimayo, a well-known restaurant and historic landmark. Here, for the first time I had the opportunity to meet more members of my birth family and to begin the long process of getting to know them more intimately. Bill Hurt and his wife, Carol, drove his father, Robert Kemper Hurt, and his wife, Opal, down from Denver. Uncle Kemper was my mother's younger brother. My father's other sister, Nellie Hernandez, arrived from Las Cruces, along with her son, Johnny, and his wife, Frances. Sam and his family came from Oklahoma. Though the reunion was brief, the luncheon, an evening at Parker's, and breakfast the next morning for everyone at a local restaurant—I came to experience the beginning of a real bonding with the family.

Aunt Louise had greatly impressed me, despite her adamant denial of blood relationship. The testimony of Aunt Carroll, of course, counterbalanced this, but Parker had always been convinced that the tension between the two families extended as far back as my mother and father's marriage. On this occasion, however, the families were certainly more than civil; in fact, they seemed genuinely to enjoy one another. If Aunt Louise had impressed me, I found myself equally impressed with Aunt Nellie, Louise's younger sister. She was a strikingly attractive woman, regal in appearance. On this occasion she wore a beautiful blue dress that offset her snow-white hair. What struck me most particularly, however, was her voice. It was deeply resonant, and she spoke in a deliberate measure, as though she was carefully weighing every word in order not to strike a false note.

Aunt Nellie's husband, John Whitlock Hernandez, died a year before my mother's death. He was a member of a distinguished Hispanic New Mexico family. His father was the first United States Representative from New Mexico when it entered the Union. For many years Uncle John and Aunt Nellie lived in Texas where he was an agent for the U. S. Internal Revenue Service. From there, until his retirement, they lived in Lima, Peru, where he served as a tax consultant for the Peruvian government. Aunt Nellie's career was no less interesting. For thirty years, before and during her marriage, she was an educator, principally as an elementary teacher, but also at one point as the master of a woodworking shop and on another occasion, the coach of a boys' basketball team.

My cousin, Dr. John Hernandez, and his wife, Frances, brought Aunt Nellie to the memorial service, and I quickly became acquainted with them as well. Johnny was a very successful civil engineer who combined his teaching at New Mexico State University with a career both as a practicing engineer and a sought-after consultant for Engineering-Science Inc. Frances had earned her doctorate in English and was a member of the Department of English at the University of Texas at El Paso. In part because they had no children, the two of them were world travelers. When Johnny received a lucrative consulting job in Thailand, Frances managed a Fulbright Grant at the same time and place, an arrangement that worked out on a number of occasions in a variety of countries. Johnny kept a close relationship with Parker; furthermore, his sister, Jean, was a contemporary of our sister, Jeanne, at the University of New Mexico. As Beverly and I began to talk with Johnny and Frances, their warmth and enthusiasm were contagious, although Frances quietly confided to me at one point then that she wasn't sure that I really was a Wells. She had no reason to deny the opinion that both her mother-in-law and her aunt conveyed. Still, both she and Johnny seemed genuinely interested in me and extended to both of us every good wish.

Thus, the Wells connection came to the memorial service from southern New Mexico and the Hurts from Colorado, and I found myself overwhelmed by the air of acceptance they displayed. Uncle Kemper had retired a few years earlier from a prestigious position at the Rocky Mountain Arsenal. His retirement had been brought on by an unfortunate heart attack stemming from the overwhelming stress created by political pressure that had been brought to bear upon the management of the arsenal. I immediately took to him. The youngest in the Hurt family, Robert Kemper, was a soft-spoken, pleasant man, very much in the mold of his older brother, Bill. He conveyed an easy, gentle sense of humor. He had obtained his engineering degree from the University of New Mexico, and, before settling down in Colorado, had traveled widely throughout the United States.

One of these stops took him to Oklahoma City, where he worked for the Phillips Petroleum Co., and where, in 1938, he met a beautiful secretary who became his wife. Although Opal was now in her eighties, there was no doubt that she had once been a real beauty, for she was still a truly attractive woman. For a time they lived in Ohio where he managed the Army's TNT plant and in Denver where he worked, first, for the Gates Rubber Co. and finally where he became the civilian in charge of nerve gas production at the arsenal. I found it ironic that as gentle a person as Uncle Kemper could at the same time oversee the production of such terrible weapons of war. We often assume that one's personality will obviously match his or her occupation, yet it is equally true that one's personality may on occasion contrast starkly with one's occupation.

At the time of the memorial service, Kemper's son, Bill, was deeply involved in land development in the Colorado Springs area. He and his wife, Carol, were every bit as personable as Johnny and Frances. It was with great pleasure that I quickly found myself at ease with the whole company.

I had now made acquaintance with a large number of both the Wells and Hurt families, and the prospects of future acquaintance excited me. Beverly and I returned shortly to Pennsylvania, determined, if possible, not only to bask in the luxury of my new family but also to extend and deepen this fascinating new relationship.

*   *   *

Over the next decade we found our desire fulfilled. Although we were not often able to meet these newfound members of my family, a number of events occurred that afforded opportunities to draw closer to them. Both Parker and Sam found it possible to travel to the East and visit us in Beaver Falls. Sam's brother-in-law lived in Washington, D. C., so Sam and Dixie spent a few days in our home before travelling on to the capital. Sam found himself scrutinizing the many road cuts around Pittsburgh, particularly on the interstate highways and the freeways. Here, he could examine first hand the geological layers that had been laid down through the ages.

Earlier, Parker told me that he was a Civil War buff; so we planned a trip in which he and Floraida would come by rail to Pittsburgh; from there we would drive to Gettysburg and thence to Washington. One project that particularly appealed to us was attempting to locate the grave of our great-grandfather, who had served in the Union Army during the Civil War. I had conducted considerable research into the life of this man and found that he was buried in Arlington National Cemetery.

Reinholt Hess was born in Hanover, Germany, January 10, 1830, and emigrated to the United States sometime before the outbreak of the Civil War. He entered the army as a private at Ft. Snelling, Minnesota, serving initially with Co. H of the First Regiment, Minnesota Infantry. He was serving in this company when he was wounded at the Battle of Gettysburg, July 2, 1863. Although another record states that he was wounded at Antietam, there exists no corroborating proof for this.

Subsequently, he served with Co. C of the 29th Illinois Volunteer Infantry and was discharged from the army May 5, 1864.

His wounds, while not fatal, must have been severe. The record states that he was shot through the lower jaw or the mouth. As I read about him, I conjectured about the emotional impact of these wounds in later years, for evidently trouble beset him throughout his life. He apparently tried farming, never living long at any one location. The record shows that he moved from Wisconsin to Kansas; from there to Utah and South Dakota, and thence to Louisiana.

His domestic life proved to be as unsuccessful as his farming. Sometime, shortly following the end of the war, Reinholt married Sophia Kleberger, probably in Wisconsin. They had two children, my grand-mother Lena, born in 1868, and George, born three years later. As stated earlier, the marriage failed; Sophia divorced Reinholt in 1873 while they lived in Kansas. She states in her petition to the court that the grounds for the divorce were that her husband was "an habitual drunkard" and "guilty of extreme cruelty towards" her. Sophia soon married Caleb Preston, a farmer, probably living near Newton, Kansas. A daughter, Nell, was born there in 1874, for whom my Aunt Nellie was named. A son, Preston, and a daughter, Elsie, followed. The family moved to Las Vegas, New Mexico, in 1881, living for a time in a tent near the Santa Fe Railway station and later in a home on Lincoln Ave.

In 1880 Reinholt married Eliza Raunts to whom was born one son in 1881, John Henry Hess. The marriage took place in Livingston Parish, Louisiana. By 1899, however, Reinholt was living in the National Soldier's Home in Milwaukee. His written statement to the Bureau of Pensions reveals that he and Eliza had separated five years earlier. Here her maiden name appears as Eliza Rohms, again a discrepancy for which there appears to be no explanation. The records show no improvement in Reinholt's life; rather, they indicate the contrary. In 1913, John H. Hess states that his father, "a pensioner under the act of 1907…is now in the insane depart-ment of this soldiers' home" in Milwaukee. Reinholt Hess died at St.

Elizabeth's Hospital, Washington, D. C., March 3, 1918. What contributed to the tortured life he had lived? I could scarcely imagine what this restless great-grandfather might have experienced, a wanderer, moving from place to place, possibly never knowing a stable home for more than a few short years, and dying ingloriously in a mental hospital.

Parker and I, following the explicit instructions given us at the office of Arlington National Cemetery, wound our way through the maze of roadways traversing the cemetery, and we eventually came upon our great-grandfather's grave. A simple stone bearing his name marks the spot. It stands in a seemingly endless row of simple stones, all of them alike. Neither Parker nor I felt any special emotion; perhaps a mild sense of triumph. We had set out on a mission and had completed it successfully. Reinholt meant little to us as a person then; he came alive only through the sheaf of records furnished me by the Office of Pensions in the Department of Interior. A tragic story by all accounts; one that may surely demonstrate the ongoing effects of war on the human soul.

Several years later, through a series of extraordinary circumstances, I came to know my great-grandfather's other, Louisiana, family, and to develop a pleasant, continuing relationship with these persons.

Although the information about Reinholt Hess proved to be the most extensive data about my forebears that I discovered to that point, the other branches of my family tree were interesting in other ways as well. These forebears, appeared in one or another document, that, when taken together, formed an exciting mosaic.

I began to fill in the sketchy outlines of my family history. Lena Henrietta Hess, a few years after arriving in Las Vegas, New Mexico, with her mother and stepfather, Caleb Preston, married Samuel Harris Wells. His father and uncle Samuel were, according to my Aunt Nellie, "freighters over the Santa Fe Trail," and their "headquarters were at Independence, Missouri." Joseph Moore White Wells was a native of New Jersey who, with his brother, prospered in the freight carrying business. According to Aunt Nellie, my great-grandmother, Louise Rucker Wells, came from Ireland when fifteen and lived during the Civil War in Virginia; however, the census of 1860 states that she was born in Missouri. Another apparent discrepancy. One seldom solves such discrepancies, so I found myself simply accepting the fact and satisfying myself with only that which I could prove. Great-grandfather Wells died at a relatively early age; his wife survived him by forty-two years. In her old age she lived in Las Vegas in a little house behind the Wells home, located on Lincoln Ave. only a short distance from the home of the Prestons. Aunt Nellie remembered her as a short woman, "inclined to be plump," always wearing "a white, starched, beautifully ironed apron over her dress." Aunt Nellie describes her as "very neat and always very, very clean." I have never found an account of how she met and married into the Wells family.

Marital difficulties often repeat themselves across the generations, and so it was with Samuel and Lena. Although they had three children, the two of them seem to have been scarcely compatible. My Aunt Louise was born in 1893, Aunt Nellie in 1896 and my father in 1898. The property on Lincoln Ave. was purchased in the name of my grandmother, indicating that she was the dominant force in the home; further, that she might well have had a less than positive regard for my grandfather's business acumen. In any event, Samuel left Lena, she then divorced him, and by 1910 he had remarried. He and his second wife had one child, Joseph, and a grandchild, Parker. (I find it fascinating that the given names—often uncommon—occur repeatedly in my family.) Frances Hernandez once told me that my father and his two sisters never met Joseph, their half-brother, until they were well into middle age, and, as late as the 1980s, none of the family had met Parker.

*   *   *

I discovered that a much more elaborate family tree existed for the Hurt family, one extending farther back in time as well. I came to know the Hurt family history and found that my great-grandmother Matilda

(Maude) Lea Fennell was born in 1847 in Huntsville, Alabama, the sixth child of Francis Marion Fennell and Isabella Allison. Originally spelled Fennelle, the family was of French Huguenot stock and followers of Peter Waldo. A brief "history" would not be inappropriate.

Following the revocation of the Edict of Nantes, Jean Victor Jules Fenelle, Count of Valois, fled to New York, where he became a successful businessman. The family eventually moved to Virginia and dropped the final "e" in their name. Jean Fenelle's great great-grandson married Elizabeth Hobbs and fathered two sons, James and Francis Marion. Both sons were surgeons, and each married one of the Allison sisters who had come to America from Londonderry, Ireland. By then both families lived near Huntsville, Alabama

Francis Marion Fennell, related to Francis Marion, known in American history as the colorful Swamp Fox of the Revolution, was the father of Matilda who married my great-grandfather, William Carroll Hurt of Nashville, Tennessee, in 1872. A veteran of the Confederate Army, he owned a coal mine in northern Alabama. The story has been handed down that when an outbreak of cholera occurred which almost cost him his life, he was ordered west, and the family moved to Los Cerrillos, New Mexico, in 1882. A more likely story states that he had a "touch of tuberculosis," the clear air of New Mexico being of great benefit.

William Carroll and Matilda Hurt had three children: my grandfather, William C., born in 1874, Mary, born in 1878, and Arthur, born in 1881. My great-grandfather lived only ten more years; at his death the family moved to Santa Fe. My great-grandmother lived there until her death on Christmas Day, 1929. Her obituary reveals that, although "a member of a prominent southern family [with a] fine old southern mansion, she had her share of adversity. She was educated privately; and then graduated from the Huntsville College for Young Women. An ardent sympathizer with the Confederacy, [she] was arrested once by a Union general for displaying her antagonism to the North by tying tiny confederate flags to the ears of cows grazing in the fields." Her father was once "strung up by an angry...squad of Union soldiers...but he escaped death by hanging...as friends released him." Later, she "dared the terrors of the wild west and...suffered...one bank failure, wiping out the savings of many years."

My grandfather Hurt, having grown up within sight of the Santa Fe Railroad, eventually moved to Las Vegas, New Mexico, an important railroad center, and became a conductor on the railroad. He married Edna Rhodes who, along with her brother Charlie, had moved with her parents, William and Ida Rhodes, to New Mexico from Caney, Kansas, sometime before 1900. Upon Ida's death, her body was returned to Caney where she lies buried. My great-grandfather remained in New Mexico until his death. Ironically, my great-uncle Charlie, the St. Louis Cardinals pitcher mentioned earlier, died in 1918, the same year as his mother, victim of the same dread epidemic.

*   *   *

During the years following my mother's memorial service I came to know other members of my family. Both Uncle Bill and Uncle Kemper fathered sons named Bill. Uncle Bill's Bill lives in Saudi Arabia, working as an engineer for ARAMCO, the huge oil company located there. He and his wife, Candy, are parents of two children, Shana and Kieran. A year or two after my initial acquaintance with the family, Uncle Bill told me that his granddaughter, Shana, had entered Duquesne University in Pittsburgh. Beverly and I had little trouble locating her and grew to love this beautiful, friendly, raven-haired cousin. Although our meetings were infrequent, we managed to see her often enough to follow her academic career with interest.

The friendship with the daughter eventually led to our meeting her father and mother, when they returned to the United States for a visit that included Pittsburgh. Again I found my cousin and his wife not only very interesting persons in themselves but also as welcoming to me as those I had already met. Shana, having graduated from Duquesne, moved to

California to be near her fiancé, Lance Toerein, a native of South Africa. When they decided to marry, they asked me to perform the ceremony. Unfortunately, I had a long-standing commitment to go abroad and was unable to fulfill Shana's request. The fact that she asked a cousin that she scarcely knew pleased me. We have continued to foster that relationship, and recently we were able to visit Shana and Lance in their home.

Because he was living in Colorado Springs, Kemper's Bill proved to be more accessible. A delightful couple, Bill and Carol Hurt presented no barrier to our getting acquainted. Because our daughter, Rebecca, continues to live in Colorado Springs, we have been able, on nearly every visit with her, to get together with Bill and Carol, sometimes through a lengthy telephone conversation but often over a meal in the setting of Bill and Carol's handsome home. Bill has pursued a very successful career in real estate. When we first met he was the "commercial agent" for a real estate development in northeast Colorado Springs. Eventually, he moved from this position and began to work for Shields Realty, one of the largest in the city, eventually becoming the sole owner. Bill and Carol are parents of three daughters and a son, one of whom, Michelle, is a well-known athlete locally, particularly for her participation in the triathlon. Bill and Carol have been avid mountain climbers. Moreover, they are strongly committed, charismatic Roman Catholics and particularly active in the marriage encounter program.

All along, we have kept in close touch with a number of family members: Parker and Floraida, Johnny and Frances Hernandez and his mother, my Aunt Nellie. In the early 90s we had the opportunity of traveling with Parker and Floraida to Ruidoso, New Mexico, to see my Aunt Carroll again. By this time she had sold her Roswell home and had moved to Ruidoso to be near her only son, Paul, and his wife, Anndy. When we first met her, Aunt Carroll had told me about Paul, but to this point I had never seen him.

Upon meeting him, I found Paul to be another warm-hearted cousin. A born outdoors man, he has written much about New Mexico ranching and has just published his fourth book. Following two brief marriages, Paul found in Anndy a delightful partner. A friendly, gregarious woman, she is a deeply committed Christian. Through her influence Paul has also become an active Christian. On this visit, then, two more members of the family opened their arms to me. We had a happy, albeit much too brief, visit, and I left Ruidoso, saddened by the realization that I might never see Aunt Carroll again in this life. Aunt Carroll died in the autumn of 2000.

*   *   *

In June of 1995, Beverly and I attended the first wedding in the immediate family since I had entered it. My nephew, Ken Wells, married Marina Salazar that day in the St. Francis Cathedral, Santa Fe. My background being exclusively Protestant, this was only the third Roman Catholic wedding I had ever witnessed. Again I was to enter into an entirely new cultural experience. I found the ceremony itself to be not so much strange as fascinating. I found myself concentrating on the differences—and similarities—to the customary Protestant ceremony. Moreover, the reception provided an even more memorable cultural experience: from the procession into the hotel ballroom, led by the bride and groom, to the abundance of food, thoroughly Hispanic, to the music that accompanied the meal and the dancing. We sat with my cousin, Johnny, and his wife, Frances, directly in front of one of the huge loudspeakers.

The amplification of the band whose repertoire consisted principally of Latin numbers made it virtually impossible to be heard; we had to shout our way through the meal yet found the joy of the occasion irresistible. We also discovered a side of Frances' personality that we never dreamed of. When the dancing began, this university professor who, although fun loving, seemed to us to be appropriately reserved, showed us that she definitely knew how to cut a rug. Neither Beverly nor I made it to the dance floor that day, nor did Johnny, but Parker, whose dancing skill I had already observed on an earlier cruise we had taken with him and Floraida, took her to the floor; then Frances. Floraida's dancing was joyous but reserved; Frances, on the other hand, cut loose in the swing style of the 1940s and jitterbugged with abandon. As I watched her, I wondered whether her students had ever seen this side of their professor.

Eventually, Johnny signaled to me to come with him, and we left the building.

"Norman," he said, "that music was getting to be too much for me. My ears can't take it. Besides, I wanted to talk with you in some quiet setting. Not shout any longer."

Johnny had a plan, so we started to walk through the center of Santa Fe.

"Let me show you something of the capital. Have you ever seen this part of Santa Fe?"

"No, but lead on." The particular area we entered was totally different from anything I'd seen in Santa Fe before.

For the next hour Johnny conducted an informal tour of the capital area, explaining the role his grandfather Hernandez had played in the state and federal government at the time New Mexico was admitted into the Union. Not totally to my surprise, he described how his grandfather had changed his political affiliation from Republican to Democrat, largely, according to Johnny, because he had become disillusioned with what he viewed as Republican corruption.

Eventually, we sat on the low wall curbing a lovely park and talked of family and writing and faith before returning to the celebration and its rousing, high-decibel joy. For me, it was a wonderful hour of conversation, quiet and satisfying.

*　　　　　　*　　　　　　*

The next year Aunt Nellie celebrated her 100th birthday. Johnny and Frances insisted that we come to Las Cruces and join in the celebration, which we did with great delight. The trip also allowed us to visit Rebecca in Colorado Springs; then Aunt Nellie. Unfortunately, a long-standing arrangement with our grandson to live with us for a week, made it impossible to be present at the actual celebration. We flew by stages from Colorado Springs to Las Cruces in planes so small that I could scarcely stand up in the cabin. We forgot all of this, however, when we visited with Aunt Nellie in the nursing home. Although the visit was brief, the conversation was thoroughly enjoyable, for she was still alert, although unable to get about on her own. It was evident that she loved and had accepted me. We knew when we kissed her good-bye that we might never see her again, nor did we. She died the following May, just short of her 101st birthday.

Although we were unable to celebrate with Aunt Nellie the next day, we greatly appreciated those quiet, personal moments with her that might not have been possible in the excitement of the actual celebration. Moreover, it was on this occasion that I was able to meet another of my first cousins. Aunt Nellie's daughter, Jean Dodier, had come from Portland, Oregon, for her mother's birthday. Jean had met her husband, Victor, when she lived in Texas. They are the parents of eight children, several of whom were present for the celebration.

Johnny had arranged for Jean, Beverly and me to dine together at La Posta in Mesilla the evening before we were to leave. As we sat for two hours in this splendid Spanish restaurant we did our best to catch up on all the past years, just as we had done with the rest of the family. Our visit with Jean proved that she possessed the same warmth of affectionate family acceptance as had the other family members. She proved to be a gracious, sweet and pleasant cousin, thoroughly interested in our lives, our children and our aspirations. After we returned to Beaver Falls, we agreed that our bond in the family had become stronger than ever.

Even more significantly, before Aunt Nellie died her role in my life assumed an importance greater than ever before. Early in 1994 I had received a letter from Frances and Johnny that finally laid to rest the mystery of my origins. Ever since Aunt Louise had declared to Beverly that I was "not a Wells," that cloud had inevitably hung over my relationship with the Wells side of the family. Parker and Aunt Carroll had continued to insist that "Buzzy" Wells was my true father, but I felt a certain reserve in my sister, Jeanne, and even from Frances and Johnny.

The letter concerned a conversation that Frances had had with her mother-in-law around Christmas, 1993. As Frances described it:

Our mother is getting very frail, bored with her condition, and praying to die. But she maintains her intelligence...she believes that she will not see you again, but she wanted us to tell you that she knows [you are] her brother's son. She said, "He is a Wells all over." She explained that she and her sister, Louise, were always ashamed to admit that their dear little brother, Samuel Harris, would be so irresponsible as to impregnate the little neighbor girl, Betty Hurt, who was ten years younger than he. And then no child appeared! It did not occur to them that you had been given away for adoption. It is, of course, a matter that has been on her mind for a long time; she wants the record straight before she dies.

I wrote to Aunt Nellie expressing my gratitude for her admission. Frances replied a few days later telling me that because I had printed the letter in "bold, black letters," she read it over and over, "obviously feeling very satisfied by it." Frances concluded her message: "We are also relieved and happy that all shadows are clear about your enclosure in the Wells tribe. The best additions anyone could imagine!"

Aunt Nellie did not die before we saw her again, and, following this "confession" from her, I became aware that the cloud of uncertainty had truly vanished; the entire Wells connection now received me into the family unconditionally.

Aunt Nellie's influence did not cease with her death. Again, through conversations with Frances and Johnny during the year following her death, I learned that my Hess forebears were Jewish. Apparently none of the living members of the Wells family knew much, if anything, about this fact until Aunt Nellie and Frances discussed it shortly before Aunt Nellie's death. Both Reinholt and Sophia were German Jews; therefore, Lena Henrietta was Jewish as well. That she and her children attended the Presbyterian Church in Las Vegas may have hidden that fact from her descendants.

Aunt Nellie, however, knew the true state of the matter. "Why," she said on one occasion to Frances, "why do you suppose Louise and I were *always* invited to the annual Chanukah festivities in Las Vegas?"

Frances admitted that she had heard something of this in the past but hadn't put two and two together.

"And why," Aunt Nellie continued, "do you think my mother was so well cared for by the Las Vegas Jewish community? The owners of the Plaza Hotel were leading members of that community," she explained. "When our father wasn't doing all that well financially, who do you think supplied the necessary money to buy the land on which we built our home?"

I remembered that the record indicated that Lena had, indeed, been the purchaser of the land.

She concluded, "Even though we worshipped as Presbyterians, when the time came that our father left Mother, the Jewish community saw to it that she never wanted for anything."

Now I understood much more than before about the Hess family and their life in the early days in Las Vegas. It was certainly one of the most intriguing genealogical facts that I came to know throughout my entire search, even though, technically, I was not Jewish myself, the line from Lena to me having come through the male side of the family. I asked myself, what next? For I had been surprised repeatedly over the years since I had first discovered my birth family. On each occasion I had been forced to rethink my heritage. On each occasion the horizons had broadened in surprising ways.

*   *   *

During my contented childhood every circumstance inculcated me to accept a set of presuppositions that, taken as a whole, defined me. Although I knew from an early age that I was an adopted child, that fact, together with all the assorted facts surrounding my birth and my birth family, meant nothing to me. I harbored no curiosity about my past; I lived in a clearly defined present, a situation that continued to govern my life for more than sixty years. When, today, I read of adoptees driven to find their biological family, often resentful that they have been reared by adoptive parents, and so desperate that in many instances they cast off those who offer them the only security they have known, I realize how different the situation has become since I was a child, and I thank God for my experience, as innocent as theirs is troubled.

Moreover, in a time when open adoptions have become commonplace, many adoptees discover something of their natural heritage very early in life, for better or worse. That an adoptee reaching the age of majority can freely visit her birth mother while retaining her adoptive status, even continuing to live with her adoptive parents, has created an entirely different set of circumstances from those in which I matured.

For me, the whole process of discovery, coming as late as it did, has been filled with excitement—a personal mystery solved through a series of events, some of them verging on the miraculous. In itself, the solving of a mystery has proven to carry with it the rush of addiction. Beyond this, as the mystery has unraveled, its denouement has produced surprises, often running counter to those presuppositions that so strongly characterized my life from childhood to maturity.

Throughout this account I have described at length many of these presuppositions. I assumed without question my Scotch-Irish heritage. Both of my adoptive parents came from this stock, and there appears to be no significant deviation from it as far back as one can trace. Once I discovered the lineage of my birth parents, I found, along with a fair amount of Scotch-Irish blood, German Jewish forbears as well as others who were of French Huguenot stock.

Until I moved from Kansas to Pennsylvania when I was sixteen, I had never met a Jew nor had I scarcely seen a Roman Catholic, let alone counted myself a friend of a person belonging to either persuasion. This circumstance changed considerably when I entered my junior year of high school, for not only did I find myself a member of a class of more than three hundred students (an increase nearly tenfold over my previous high school class) but I also "rubbed shoulders" with many students from ethnic backgrounds I had never heard of before—most of them Catholic or Orthodox and among them more than a handful of Jews. Although many of these students became friends, my closest associations, with rare exception, remained Protestant. During my subsequent life, little changed in this regard, until I found myself drawn into my new family. Here I found a range of religious profession I had never known intimately before, from Presbyterian and Methodist to Unitarian and Roman Catholic. Overnight, as it were, I found that my newly discovered family had inevitably broadened my perspective and forced me to rethink my attitude toward others of a different religious conviction.

Throughout my childhood I identified with the plains states of the Midwest; then I moved to the Mid-Atlantic region where I have lived, with the exception of very brief periods, ever since. My fondness for the mountain states was established early on, but I was never to live there at any time. The discovery of my birth family brought me, most directly, into the American Southwest, specifically New Mexico. Before my first encounter with my brother, Parker, I had driven only once through that state. Since my coming to know my family I have, on several occasions, been delighted to become acquainted with the "land of enchantment" first hand and to come to love it.

Digging into the past, moreover, I have uncovered two further geographic "roots." One of these simply reinforces my Northern orientation: family migration from New Jersey, Wisconsin, Minnesota, Illinois; finally to Kansas, where I grew up oblivious to their presence. The other root, however, is totally Southern: a migration from New York to Virginia,

North Carolina, Georgia, Alabama, Tennessee, and finally to New Mexico. Additionally, a part of the northern root eventually became established in Louisiana. So, while I have never spent any considerable time in the South, have never set foot in Alabama or Mississippi, I have family, still thoroughly southern, with whom I have at least come into contact since the unfolding of my family began.

Moreover, my southern heritage brings with it an entire range of possibilities—call them rebel possibilities if you like—that I had no way of even suspecting throughout the years. It is a commonplace to speak of brother fighting brother in the War Between the States. I have come to see that, although this particular tragedy never occurred in my family, my great-grandfather Hess and my great-grandfather Hurt fought on opposite sides in that conflict. I assume, likewise, that what one might describe as Southern sensibility also lies behind a great portion of my family—gracious living, noblesse oblige, breeding, gentility—all those matters that we like to associate with the Old South. How much of that was bled out of those who moved west and endured the rigors of the frontier is impossible to measure. From the stories that I have been told, the aristocratic streak endured, especially among the women who lived and died in New Mexico. They are the ones who made sure that their lineage extended back to the Revolution and became members of the D.A.R. In this connection it strikes me as ironic that the descendants of this "aristocratic" Southern branch occupied a less privileged status in Las Vegas than did the more bourgeois descendants who were their neighbors. At the time of my parents' marriage, there was a distinct feeling by the Wellses that their Harry had married "beneath" him.

It also came as a surprise to find that many of my family were as partial to the Democrat Party as I was to the Republican. This loyalty of theirs, like mine, was unquestioned. If I had thought about this more carefully, I would have realized that the Southern branch of my family would have almost certainly been Democrat loyalists. After all, they lived in a South untouched by the Yankee migration that has produced the New South.

Furthermore, my New Mexico family were as disenchanted by what they perceived to be state-wide Republican corruption as I had been by my own anti-Democrat perceptions.

Here, then, I found myself as the process of discovery expanded to its conclusion: Scotch-Irish, but also German and French; Protestant with numerous Roman Catholic relatives; Southern Rebel as well as Yankee; tied closely to the American Southwest as much as to the Northeast; and politically ambivalent. There remained one final fascinating piece to fit into this mosaic.

Since the mid-nineteenth century the question of nature versus nurture has become a topic of endless discussion. These theories advocating the powerful influence of one or the other of these two forces have gained wide acceptance. Nature or nurture? I cannot claim any divine insight into the question, nor can I advance conclusive evidence that might weigh more heavily on one or the other side. I can only describe what I find to be true in my personal experience.

My childhood and adolescence, described earlier, clearly reflect the influence of my adoptive mother and father and various other members of my immediate adoptive family. For the most part they were educators, all of them with some college education, most of them graduates. Thus, I matured in a literary milieu, books forming the bulk of my birthday presents through all my early years. When I emerged from the halls of academe I first took the path to the pastoral ministry but eventually to the teaching of English literature. Until I discovered my birth family I had assumed without question that my interests and eventually my calling were largely if not totally the result of the nurturing influences of my youth.

I was amazed to find that, among my immediate family, counting first cousins, no fewer than ten individuals out of nineteen were either teachers or writers. This percentage, while perhaps not overwhelming, certainly challenged my long-held assumption. When I added to this number other members of the family who were not in these professions but were highly educated and successful members of society, I began to realize just what the possibility of genetic influence might actually be.

*   *   *

When I weigh the experiences that constitute the search for and discovery of my birth family against the risks one might meet in such an undertaking, I have no doubt at all that in my case the entire process has been a positive one. My birth family might have rebuffed me; instead, I have been accepted at every turn. I have also found that this acceptance has been conveyed with warmth and enthusiasm. I might have found the various leads I had to follow petering out, leading to frustration and eventually to my abandoning the whole process. Instead, each lead followed provided another colorful thread in the family tapestry. On the other hand, I might have found the newly discovered family so exciting, so impressive, that my adoptive family would fade by comparison. Not so. The Carson family who nurtured me remain every bit as much my family as before. Instead, I have two families now, one with whom I identify because of the more than six decades of maturing within their circle, and the other who have opened up the new vistas, described earlier, vistas that compel me to reexamine my very being.

Certain traits are, of course, ingrained within me, but, because of another perspective, in many ways quite new to me, I have been forced to take a more accepting stance in a number of areas: political, religious, ethnic, and cultural. We must not confuse tolerance with indifference, however, and I find that much of my early instruction—my faith commitment principally—has not changed. In that sense I am not indifferent to the diversity that I have come to discover. Yet that diversity has come to add considerable color to a life that I assumed was already as colorful as might be expected.

Perhaps the most striking lesson that has impressed itself upon me involves the concept of adoption. From my early intimate acquaintance with the Bible I became aware of the Christian doctrine of adoption: that the Sovereign God not only justifies the sinful creature through his Son, Jesus Christ, but also initiates the work of sanctification in that person and adopts the sinner into his family. The apostle Paul makes this doctrine quite clear when he writes, "He predestined us to adoption as sons through Jesus Christ to Himself, according to the kind intention of His will, to the praise of the glory of His grace which He freely bestowed on us in the Beloved" (Ephesians 1: 5-6).

As a child of no more than ten, I set out to memorize the entire Westminster Shorter Catechism, and for that concentrated effort I received a brand new Bible. This catechism is, of course, a short, easily memorized compendium of Christian doctrine. One question has to do with the effective call of God on the individual and what benefits that call has upon the new believer. One of these important benefits is adoption. The divines describe adoption thus: "...an act of God's free grace, whereby we are received into the number, and have a right to all the privileges, of the sons of God."

I knew intellectually long ago what this doctrine of Scripture meant to me spiritually. Throughout the years I became more assured of its benefits. Of course, I eventually preached on the relevant Bible passages to my congregation. The full impact, however, of what this doctrine meant to me *physically*, as it were, came only when I discovered my physical roots, my genetic heritage and my fascinating cultural background.

With absolutely no contribution on my part to the process, I had passed out of my birth family and into my adoptive family. Why? There are stories, of course, that give some clue about the circumstances. My aunt, who alone of all that generation seemed to know more of my mother's actual story, gave me some hints: the relative poverty of my parents, the need for my father to continue his accounting course, that my mother was unable to nurse me, and the further fact that I was a sickly baby—all of these contributed probably to the decision to give me up for adoption.

Aunt Carroll had also supplied a fascinating morsel of information, presumably factual. At least she was convinced of its authenticity.

"Your mother," she said, "was offered the chance to choose the potential adoptive parents." She continued, "Betty would never know their names, but it was, I guess, a generic choice based on their occupation or profession."

"Did she do it?"

"Yes, she said that she did."

"And?"

"She chose the minister and his wife."

"And apparently she got her wish." What a miracle, I thought.

"Yes," Aunt Carroll said, "That's what she always told me she had done. She got her wish, although she was never sure that it happened that way until you wrote to her."

"How extraordinary!" I remembered Parker's having told me that my mother had expressed the wish to him, years later, to find out exactly what had happened to her first born. Only months, then, before her death she finally found out, and, from what Aunt Carroll told me, she was overjoyed in her at last knowing of my fate.

Now, as I look at the whole affair, I must believe, more strongly than ever, that God's providential hand was at work. It would be presumptuous of me to declare unequivocally that I would never have become a believing Christian had I not been adopted. Who can ever know what providential influences might have come my way? Still, from all that I have been told, it is undeniable that my birth parents were at best only marginally interested in a living faith. My adoptive parents, on the other hand, were deeply committed Christians. What would have been the dominating influences during my youth, had I remained in New Mexico? No one can tell for sure, nor will I offer a categorical opinion.

The whole process, from my birth and subsequent adoption to my finding my birth family, lies under the hand of God. I must accept His plan for my life precisely for what it has been. While I am eternally grateful to God for placing me, with no choice on my part and only a minimal choice on my mother's part, in the particular adoptive family who reared me, I am also thrilled that, in God's providence I found my wonderful birth family. For many the discovery of the birth family has been fraught with pain, often with rejection, but for me it has been the best of both worlds. For that I praise Him who brought it all about.

About the Author

Dr. Norman Carson is Professor Emeritus of English at Geneva College, Beaver Falls, Pennsylvania, where he chaired the department for twelve years. He has written articles and reviews for *Christianity and Literature, Christian Scholar's Review, Table Talk* and the *Covenanter Witness.* Currently he is the managing editor of the *Geneva Magazine.* He is an ordained minister in the Reformed Presbyterian Church of North America.

Printed in the United States
2138

9473 35

9 780595 199730